MEMORIES AND VAGARIES

BY AXEL MUNTHE

AUTHOR OF "THE STORY OF SAN MICHELE," ETC.

"Chacun ne doit raconter que ce qu'il
a vu lui-même; de cette façon le monde
connaîtra la vérité."

NEW YORK
E. P. DUTTON & CO., INC.

MEMORIES AND VAGARIES :: FIRST PUBLISHED
IN THE UNITED STATES OF AMERICA
BY E. P. DUTTON & COMPANY, INC. :: 1930

FIRST PRINTING ....NOVEMBER, 1930
SECOND PRINTING ....NOVEMBER, 1930
THIRD PRINTING ....NOVEMBER, 1930
FOURTH PRINTING ....NOVEMBER, 1930
FIFTH PRINTING ....NOVEMBER, 1930
SIXTH PRINTING ....NOVEMBER, 1930
SEVENTH PRINTING ....NOVEMBER, 1930
EIGHTH PRINTING ....NOVEMBER, 1930
NINTH PRINTING ....NOVEMBER, 1930
TENTH PRINTING ....NOVEMBER, 1930
ELEVENTH PRINTING ....NOVEMBER, 1930
TWELFTH PRINTING ....NOVEMBER, 1930

TO

R. B. CUNNINGHAME GRAHAM

FROM HIS FRIEND AND ADMIRER

PREFACE TO THE
THIRD ENGLISH
EDITION

BENEVOLENT readers of *The Story of San Michele*
have come forth with a gallant attempt to rescue
this little book from oblivion. I fear I have not
done very well for myself by consenting to a re-
print of these small sketches or stories, or whatever
they are to be called. They were all written long,
long ago by an inexperienced hand in rather indifferent English. I flatter myself with the belief
that, were I to sit down and rewrite them to-day, I
would make a better book, at least to the majority
of its readers. But there still exists a minority of
booklovers with a sneaking weakness for sponta-
neous writing, who will, maybe, approve of my boldness in leaving these stories just as they were written, to take care of themselves as best they can.

Readers of *The Story of San Michele* will come
across several old acquaintances here, all in their
same old clothes, for they have nothing else to put
on their backs. My friend Archangelo Fusco, the
street-sweeper of Quartier Montparnasse; the Salvatore family; Don Gaetano, the organ-grinder

with his shivering monkey; Monsieur Alfredo with
the MS. of his last five-act tragedy under his arm,
are all here. Even Sœur Philomène, the sweet guardian angel of Salle St. Claire in the Paris hospital,
lives and dies in these pages. The same shabby old
monks and priests are carrying through the cholera-
slums of Naples their respective madonnas and
patron saints, all quarrelling among themselves.
The same glorious sun is shining over Golfo di
Napoli. Out of its sparkling waters rises the same
enchanted island, where the same friendly people
welcome the reader. Even the dogs in this book
are wagging their tails in token of recognition. The
beloved Tappio in the chapter "When Tappio was
lost" in this book was the great-grandfather of the
Tappio Miss Hall took for his daily walk in Villa
Borghese, and who lay half-asleep in the sunny
pergola of San Michele while Billy, the drunkard
baboon, was busy catching his fleas. The pedigree
of Billy is more obscure, though I still stick to my
belief that he was an illegitimate son of Il Demonio.
But I know for certain that the wooden horse I
gave on Christmas Day to John, the blue-eyed little boy in *The Story of San Michele,* was a lineal
descendant of the wooden horse which Petrucchio,
the child of sorrow of the Salvatore family, is holding in his withered hand in this book. I know, too,
that my friend Archangelo Fusco, the street-
sweeper in Impasse Roussel, is the same Archangelo
Fusco I met in Heaven in the last chapter of the

book of San Michele. I am equally certain that his cruel landlord, the money-lender to the poor in Impasse Roussel, whom I caused to hang himself in this book, is now keeping company in hell with the ex-butcher who blinded the quails with a red-hot needle in *The Story of San Michele.*

Memories and Vagaries have been out of print for long. Death was due to natural cause, and the few mourners who accompanied the book to the common grave of oblivion, have so far borne their loss with stubborn resignation. So have I, until the long-forgotten book was read to me the other day by a friendly voice. As I listened with a compassionate smile on my lips to these humble stories, I suddenly felt a pang in my heart, and I wished I could write to-day just such a book as this with all its shortcomings, its boyish boisterousness, its guileless self-consciousness, its incorrigible *joie de vivre* and its unshaken faith. Alas! I shall wish it in vain, it is my youth I wish for!

> La vie s'en va, Madame, la vie s'en va!
> Hélas! la vie non, mais nous, nous en allons.

St. James' Club,
August, 1930.

CONTENTS

PUBLISHERS' NOTE

The first English Edition of "Memories and Vagaries" was published in London in 1898. This book is now published for the first time in any form in the United States.

MEMORIES AND VAGARIES

I

For Those Who Love Music

I HAD engaged him by the year. Twice a week he came and went through his whole *répertoire,* and lately, out of sympathy for me, he would play the Miserere of the "Trovatore," which was his show piece, twice over. He stood there in the middle of the street looking steadfastly up at my windows while he played, and when he had finished he would take off his hat with an "Addio, Signor!"

It is well known that the barrel-organ, like the violin, gets a fuller and more sympathetic tone the older it is. The old artist had an excellent instrument, not of the modern noisy type which imitates a whole orchestra with flutes and bells and beats of drums, but a melancholy old-fashioned barrel-organ which knew how to lend a dreamy mystery to the gayest *allegretto,* and in whose proudest *tempo di Marcia* there sounded an unmistakable undertone of resignation. And in the tenderer pieces of the *répertoire,* where the melody, muffled and

9

staggering like the voice of an old street-singer, groped its way amongst the rusty pipes of the treble, then there was a tremolo in the bass like suppressed sobs. Now and then the voice of the tired organ failed it completely, and then the old man would resignedly turn the handle to some bars of rest more touching than any music in their eloquent silence.

True the instrument was in itself very responsive, but the old man surely had his personal share in the sadness which came over me whenever I heard his music. He had his beat in the poor quarter behind the Jardin des Plantes, and many times during my solitary rambles up there had I stopped and taken my place among the scanty audience of ragged street boys which surrounded him.

We made acquaintance one misty, dark autumn day. I sat on a bench under the fading trees, which in vain had tried to deck the gloomy square with a little summer, and now hopelessly suffered their leaves to fall; and, like a melancholy accompaniment to my dreary thoughts, the old barrel-organ in the slum close by coughed out the aria from the last act of the "Traviata": *Addio del passato bei sogni ridenti!*

I started as the music stopped. The old man had gone through his whole *répertoire,* and after a despairing inspection of his audience he resignedly tucked the monkey under his cloak and prepared to be off. I have always liked barrel-organs, and I have a sufficiently correct ear to distinguish good music from bad; so I went up and thanked him, and asked him to play a little longer, unless he was too tired in the arm. I am afraid he was not spoiled by praise, for he looked at me with a sad, incredulous expression which pained me, and with an almost shy hesitation he asked me if it was any special piece I wished to hear. I left the choice to the old man. After a mysterious manipulation with some screws under the organ, which was answered from its depths by a half-smothered groan, he began slowly and with a certain solemnity to turn the handle, and with a friendly glance at me, he said, "Questo è per gli amici." [1]

It was a tune I had not heard him play before, but I well knew the sweet old melody, and half aloud I searched my memory for the words of perhaps the finest folk-song of Naples:

"Fenestra che luciva e mò non luce
    Segn' è ca Nenna mia stace malata
    S'affaccia la sorella e me lo dice:

"Nennella toja è morta e s'è aterrata
    Chiagneva sempe ca dormeva sola,
    Mò dorme in distìnta compagnia."

He looked at me with a shy interest while he played, and when he had finished he bared his grey

[1] "This is for friends."

head; I returned his greeting, and thus our acquaintance was made.

It was not difficult to see that times were hard
—the old man's clothes were doubtful, and the
pallor of poverty lay over his withered features,
where I read the story of a long life of failure. He
came from the mountains round Monte Cassino,
so he informed me, but where the monkey hailed
from I never quite got to know.

Thus we met from time to time during my
rambles in the poor quarters. Had I a moment to
spare I stopped for a while to listen to a tune or
two, as I saw that it gratified the old man, and
since I always carried a lump of sugar in my pocket
for any casual dog acquaintance, I soon made
friends with the monkey also. The relations between
the little monkey and her *impresario* were unusually
cordial, and this notwithstanding that she had completely failed to fulfil the expectations which had
been founded upon her—she had never been able
to learn a single trick, the old man told me. Thus
all attempts at education had long ago been
abandoned, and she sat there huddled together on
her barrel-organ and did nothing at all. Her face
was sad, like that of most animals, and her thoughts
were far away. But now and then she woke up
from her dreams, and her eyes could then take a
suspicious, almost malignant expression, as they
lit upon some of the street boys who crowded round

her tribune and tried to pull her tail, which stuck out from her little gold-laced garibaldi. To me she was always very amiable; confidently she laid her wrinkled hand in mine, and absently she accepted the little attentions I was able to offer her. She was very fond of sweetmeats, and burnt almonds were, in her opinion, the most delectable thing in the world.

Since the old man had once recognised his musical friend on the balcony of the Hôtel de l'Avenir, he often came and played under my windows. Later an agreement was made that he should come regularly and play twice a week—it may, perhaps, seem somewhat extravagant for one who was studying medicine, but the old man's terms were so moderate, and you know I have always been so fond of music. Besides, it was the only recreation at hand—I was working hard in the Hôtel de l'Avenir, for I was to take my degree in the spring.

So passed the autumn, and the hard time came. The rich tried on the new winter fashions, and the poor shivered with the cold. Well-gloved hands seemed more and more reluctant to leave the warm muff or the fur-lined pocket to pull out the penny, and more and more desperate became the struggle for bread amongst the problematical existences of the street. Before the hopelessly closed windows of the courtyard, harpists, "Zampognari," and violinists performed, unnoticed, the most pleading pieces of their *répertoire* about "La bella Napoli" and "Santa Lucia," while stiffened fingers twanged the guitar, and the little sister, shivering with cold, banged the tambourine. In vain the old street-singer sang with hoarse pathos the song about "La Gloire" and "La Patrie," and in vain my friend played that piece "per gli amici"—thicker and thicker fell the snowflakes over the humbly bared heads, and scarcer and scarcer fell the coppers into the outstretched hats.

Now and then I came across my friend, and we always had, as before, a kind word for one another. He was now wrapped up in an old Abruzzi cloak, and I noticed that the more the cold increased the more rapid became the *tempo* with which he wound out his pieces; and towards December the Miserere itself was taken in allegretto.

The monkey was now in plain clothes, and had wrapped her thin little body in a long ulster such as Englishmen wear; but she was fearfully cold notwithstanding, and, forgetful of all etiquette, more and more often she would sneak down from the barrel-organ and disappear under the old man's cloak.

. And while they were suffering out there in the cold I sat at home in my cosy, warm room, and instead of helping them, I forgot all about them, more and more absorbed as I was by my approaching examination, with no other thought than for

myself. And then one day I suddenly left my
lodgings and removed to the Hôtel Dieu to replace
a comrade, and weeks passed before I put my foot
out of the hospital. I remember it so well, it was
the very New Year's Day we met each other again.
I was crossing the Place de Notre Dame, mass was
just over, and the people were streaming out of
the old cathedral.

As usual, a row of beggars was standing before
the door, imploring the charity of the churchgoers.
The severe winter had increased their number, and
besides the usual beggars, cripples, and blind, who
were always by the church porch, reciting in loud
voices the history of their misfortune, there stood
a silent rank of Poverty's accidental recruits—poor
fellows whose daily bread had been buried under
the snow, and whose pride the cold had at last
benumbed. At the farther end, and at some distance
from the others, an old man stood with bent head
and outstretched hat, and with painful surprise I
recognised my friend in his threadbare old coat
without the Abruzzi cloak, without the barrel-
organ, without the monkey. My first impulse was
to go up to him, but an uneasy feeling of I do not
know what held me back; I felt that I got red in
the face and I did not move from my place. Every
now and then a passer-by stopped for a moment
and made as if to search his pocket, but I did not
see a single copper fall into the old man's hat.

The place became gradually deserted, and one beggar after another trotted off with his little earnings. At last a child came out of the church, led by a gentleman in mourning; the child pointed towards the old man, and then ran up to him and laid a silver coin in his hat. The old man humbly bowed his head in thanks, and in my absentmindedness I was very nearly thanking the little donor myself, so pleased was I. My friend carefully wrapped up the precious gift in an old pocket-handkerchief, and stooping forward as if still carrying the barrel-organ on his back, he walked off.

I happened to be quite free that morning, and, thinking that a little stroll before luncheon would help to shake off the atmosphere of the hospital, I followed him slowly across the Seine. Once or twice I nearly caught him up, and all but tapped him on the shoulder, with a "Buon giorno, Don Gaetano!" Yet, without exactly knowing why, I drew back at the last moment and let him get a few paces ahead of me again.

An icy wind blew straight against us, and I drew my fur cloak closer round me. But just then I suddenly asked myself why, after all, it was I who owned such a warm and comfortable fur coat, whilst the old man who tramped along in front of me had only a threadbare old jacket? And why was it for me that luncheon was waiting, and not

for him? Why should I have a good blazing fire
burning in my cosy room, while the old man had
to wander about the streets the whole day long to
find his food, and in the evening go home to his
miserable garret and, unprotected against the cold
of the winter's night, prepare for the next day's
struggle for bread?

And it suddenly dawned upon me why I had
got red in the face when I saw him at Notre Dame,
and why I could not make up my mind to go and
speak to him. I felt ashamed before this old man,
I felt ashamed at life's unmerited generosity to me
and its severity to him. I felt as if I had taken something from him which I ought to restore to him;
and I began to wonder whether it might be the fur
coat. But I got no further in my meditations, for
the old man stopped and looked in at a shop
window. We had just crossed the Place Maubert
and turned into the Boulevard St. Germain; the
boulevard was full of people, so that, without being
noticed, I could approach him quite closely. He was
standing before a smart confectioner's shop, and
to my surprise he entered without hesitation. I took
up my position before the shop window, alongside
some shivering street arabs who stood there, absorbed in the contemplation of the unattainable
delicacies within, and I watched the old man carefully untie his pocket-handkerchief and lay the little

girl's gift upon the counter. I had hardly time to
draw back before he came out with a red paper bag
of sweets in his hand, and with rapid steps he
started off in the direction of the Jardin des
Plantes.

I was very much astonished at what I had seen,
and my curiosity made me follow him. He
slackened his pace at one of the little slums behind
Hôpital de la Pitié, and I saw him disappear into
a dirty old house. I waited outside a minute or two,
and then I groped my way through the pitch-dark
entrance, climbed up a filthy staircase, and found
a door slightly ajar. An icy, dark room, in the
middle three ragged little children crouched together around a half-extinct brazier, in the corner
the only furniture in the room—a clean iron bed-
stead, with crucifix and rosary hung on the wall
above it, and by the window an image of the
Madonna adorned with gaudy paper flowers; I
was in Italy, in my poor exiled Italy. And in the
purest Tuscan the eldest sister informed me that
Don Gaetano lived in the garret. I went up there
and knocked, but no one answered, so I opened the
door myself. The room was brightly lit up by a
blazing fire. With his back towards the door, Don
Gaetano was on his knees before the stove busy
heating a little saucepan over the fire, beside him
on the floor lay an old mattress with the well-known
Abruzzi cloak thrown over it, and close by, spread

out on a newspaper, were various delicacies—an
orange, walnuts, and raisins, and there also was
the red paper bag. Don Gaetano dropped a lump
of sugar into the saucepan, stirred it with a stick,
and in a persuasive voice I heard him say, "Che
bella roba, che bella roba, quanto è buono questa
latte con lo zucchero! Non piange anima mia,
adesso siamo pronti!" [1]

A slight rustling was heard beneath the Abruzzi
cloak, and a black little hand was stretched out
towards the red paper bag.

"Primo il latte, primo il latte," admonished the
old man. "Non importa, piglia tu una," [2] he re-
pented, and took a big burnt almond out of the
paper bag; the little hand disappeared, and a
crunching was heard under the cloak. Don Gaetano
poured the warm milk in a saucer, and then he carefully lifted up a corner of the cloak. There lay the
poor little monkey with heaving breast and eyes
glowing with fever. Her face had become so small,
and her complexion was ashy grey. The old man
took her on his knees, and tenderly as a mother he
poured some spoonfuls of the warm milk into her
mouth. She looked with indifferent eyes towards
the delicacies on the table, and absently she let her
fingers pass through her master's beard. She was

---

[1] "What nice things, what nice things, how good this milk with
sugar is! Don't cry, my darling, it is ready now!"
[2] "The milk first, the milk first—never mind, take one."

so tired that she could hardly hold her head up, and now and then she coughed so that her thin little body shook, and she pressed both her hands to her temples. Don Gaetano shook his head sadly, and carefully laid the little invalid back under the cloak.

A feeble blush spread over the old man's face as he caught sight of me. I told him I happened to be passing by just as he was entering his house, and that I took the liberty of following him upstairs in order to bid him good morning and to give him my new address, in the hope that he would come and play to me as before. Involuntarily I looked round for the barrel-organ as I spoke, and Don Gaetano, who understood, informed me that he no longer played the organ—he sang. I glanced at the precious pile of wood beside the fireplace, at the new blanket that hung before the window to keep out the draught, at the delicacies on the newspaper—and I also understood.

The monkey had been ill three weeks—"la febbre," explained the old man. We knelt one at each side of the bed, and the sick animal looked at me with her mute prayer for help. Her nose was hot, as it is with sick children and dogs, her face wrinkled like that of an old, old woman, and her eyes had got quite a human expression. Her breathing was so short, and we could hear how it rattled in her throat. The diagnosis was not difficult—she had consumption. Now and again she stretched out her thin arms as if she implored us to help her, and Don Gaetano thought that she did so because she wished to be bled.[1] I would willingly have given in in this case, although opposed in principle to this treatment, if I had thought it possible that any benefit could have been derived from it; but I knew only too well how unlikely this was, and I tried my best to make Don Gaetano understand it. Unhappily I did not know myself what could be done. I had at that time a friend amongst the keepers of the monkey-house in the Jardin des Plantes, and the same night he came with me to have a look at her; he said that there was nothing to be done, and that there was no hope. And he was right. For one week more the fire blazed in Don Gaetano's garret, then it was left to go out, and it became cold and dark as before in the old man's home.

True, he got his barrel-organ out from the pawnshop, and now and then a copper did fall into his hat also. He did not die of starvation, and that was about all he asked of life.

So the spring came and I left Paris; and God knows what has become of Don Gaetano.

If you happen to hear a melancholy old barrel-organ in the courtyard, go to the window and give

[1] The lower classes in Italy still use bleeding for all kinds of diseases, and this treatment is also extended to animals. I knew a monkey in Naples who was bled twice.

a penny to the poor errant musician—perhaps it
is Don Gaetano! If you find that his organ disturbs
you, try if you like it better by making him stand
a little further off, but don't send him away with
harshness! He has to hear so many hard words as
it is; why should not we then be a little kind to
him—we who love music?

CHAPTER II

TOYS FROM THE PARIS HORIZON

II

Toys from the Paris Horizon

In Paris the New Year is awakened by the laughter of children, the dawn of its first day glows in rosy joy on small round cheeks, and lit up by the light from children's sparkling eyes the curtain rises upon the fairy world of toys.

This world of toys is a faithful miniature of our own. The same unceasing evolution, the same struggle for existence goes on there as here. Types rise and vanish just as with us; the strongest and best-fitted individuals survive, defying time, whilst the weaker and less gifted are supplanted and die out.

To the former belongs the doll, whose individual type centuries may have modified, but whose idea is eternal, whose soul lives on with the imperishable youth of the gods. The doll is thousands of years old; it has been found in the graves of little Roman children, and the archæologists of coming generations will find it among the remains of our culture. The children of Pompeii and Herculaneum used to trundle hoops just as you and I did when we were

25

small, and who knows whether the rocking-horse on which we rode as boys is not a lineal descendant of that proud charger into whose wooden flanks the children of Francis I. dug their heels. The drum is also exempt from all modification of time; through centuries it has beaten the Christmas and New Year's day's *reveille* in the nursery to the battles of the tin-soldiers, and it will continue to beat as long as there are boys' arms to wield the drumsticks and grown-up people's tympanums to be deafened. The tin-soldier views the future with calm; he will not surrender until the day of general disarmament, and the utopia of universal peace is still far distant. Neither will the toy-sword disappear; it is the nursery-symbol of our ineradicable lust for fighting. Foolscap-crowned and bell-ringing harlequins will also defy time; they will flourish in the world of toys as long as fools are to be found in our world. Gold-laced knights with big swords at their sides, curly-locked princesses with satin shoes on dainty feet, stalwart musketeers with top boots and big moustachios—all are types which still hold their own pretty well. The Japanese doll is as yet young, but a brilliant future lies before her.

Amongst the toy-people who are gradually losing ground may be mentioned monks, hobgoblins, and kings—an evil omen for the matter of that. I don't wish to make any one uneasy, but it is a fact that the demand for kings has considerably decreased of late—my studies in toy-anthropology do not permit me the slightest doubt on the subject. It is not for me to try to explain the cause of this serious phenomenon—I understand well that this topic is a painful one, and shall not persist.

Hobgoblins—who in our world are growing more and more ill at ease since the locomotives began to pant through the forests, and who have sought and found a refuge in the toy-world, in picture-books, and fairy-tales—do not leap from their boxes with the same wild energy as they used to do, and do not know how to inspire the terror of old. They are doomed to extinction; a few generations more and wet-nurses and nursery-maids will be studying physics, and then there will be an end to hobgoblins and Jack-in-the-boxes! For my part I shall regret them.

Each generation writes the history of its civilisation in the books of its children. Our age is the age of scientific inquiry; the children of to-day have no time for dreams, and move in quite another world of thought than we used to do. Nowadays Tom Thumb is left to take care of himself in the trackless forest, and poor Robinson Crusoe, with whom we kept such faithful company, is feeling more and more lonely on his desert island with our mutual friend Friday and the patient goat whose neck we so often patted in our dreams. Nowadays boy-thoughts travel with Phileas Fogg in Jules Verne's *Round the World in Eighty Days,* or embark fearlessly on a journey to the moon with carefully calculated pace of I don't know how many miles a second, and their knapsacks stuffed with physical science. Nowadays a little future Edison sits pondering in his nursery laboratory, trying to stun a fly beneath the bell of a little air-pump, or he communicates with his little sister by means of a lilliputian telephone. All we knew was how to besiege toy-fortresses with pop-guns and bring our rival armies of tin-soldiers into action, limiting our scientific inquiries to that bloodless vivisection which consisted in ripping up the stomachs of all our dolls and pulling to pieces everything we came across to find out what was inside. These scientific toys were almost unknown some ten years ago—these *jouets scientifiques* which now rank so high in toyshops, and offer perhaps the greatest attraction for the children of to-day. *La tranquillité des parents et l'instruction des enfants* is the device on these toys—yes, there is no doubt that the children's instruction has been thought of, but their imagination, what is to become of that, now that even Christmas presents give lessons in chemistry and physics? And all this artificially increased modern thirst for knowledge, does it not dispel that poetry of rosy dreams which is the morning glow of awakening thought? Maybe

I am wrong, but it sometimes seems to me that there is less laughter in the nurseries now than in old days, that the children's faces are growing more earnest. And if I am to be quite frank, I must confess that I fight rather shy of these modern toys, and have never bought any of them for my little friends.

To the political convulsions which now and then agitate our own world can be traced the political unrest which pervades the world of toys—the swell after the storm. The political agitations of the toy-world form a mighty and hitherto rather neglected topic, far too vast, however, to be dealt with in these pages. I therefore think it well to limit myself to the French toy-politics after *l'anneé terrible* (1870-71). The war between Germany and France is over long ago, but the toy-world still resounds with the echo of the clash of arms of 1870; fighting still continues with unabated ardour in the lilliputian world, where the Bismarcks and the Moltkes of the German toy manufactories each Christmas fight new battles with *l'Article de Paris*.

Victorious by virtue of their cheapness, the Germans advance. From the Black Forest emigrate every Christmas millions of wooden oxen, sheep, horses, and dogs, to confront rival hordes which descend from the wood-carvers' factories in the Vosges (St. Claude, etc., etc.). Each Christmas thousands of dolls start for Paris from Hamburg,

Nuremberg, and Berlin to compete with their French colleagues, and each Christmas dense squadrons of spike-helmeted Prussian tin-soldiers cross the Rhine to invade the toyshops and nurseries of France. The struggle is too unequal, the competition too great. Siebenburgen and Tyrol furnish at will a complete chemist's shop, a plentifully supplied grocery, or a well-stocked farm with crops and implements, cows, sheep, and goats, grazing on the verdant pasture, for three francs fifty centimes. Hamburg at the same moderate price offers a doll irreproachable to the superficial observer, a doll with glass eyes, curly hair, and one change of clothes, whilst the little Parisienne has already spent double that sum on her toilet alone, and therefore cannot consent to be yours for less than half a louis d'or. Nuremberg mobilises a whole regiment of tin-soldiers, baggage waggons, and artillery (Krupp model) included, at the same price for which the toy-arsenals of Marais can only equip one single battalion of *Chasseurs d'Afrique.*

The outlook is gloomy—the French retire all along the line.

But France will never be annihilated! And were you to sound the depths of the French tin-soldier's soul, you would find hidden under the reserve exacted by discipline, the same glorious dream of revenge which inspired the volunteers raised from out of the earth by Gambetta. The French tin-soldier looks towards the east; he knows that he is still powerless to check the invasion of the barbarians—he is bound by Article 4 in the Frankfort Treaty of Peace, but he bides his time.[1]

And Revenge is near. This time also the signal for rising has been given from Belleville, by a Gambetta of the toy-world. Some years ago a poor workman at Belleville got a sudden inspiration, an inspiration that since then has engendered an army which would realise the dream of eternal peace, and keep in check the assembled troops of all Europe were it a question of number alone. He sets on foot 5,000,000 soldiers a year. The origin of these soldiers is humble, but so was Napoleon's. They spring from old sardine boxes. Thrown away on the dustheap, the sardine box is saved from annihilation by the dustman, who sells it to a rag-merchant in Belleville or Buttes Chaumont, who in his turn disposes of it to a specialist, who prepares it for the manufactories. The warriors are cut out from the bottom of the box. The lids and sides are used for making guns, railway-carriages, ambulances, etc., etc. All this may seem very unimportant to you at first sight, but in Belleville a large manufactory has been founded on this idea of utilising old sardine boxes, which occupies no less than two hundred workmen and produces every year over

[1] The German toys only pay, since 1871, the duty of 60 frs. per 100 kilo.

two milliards of tin toys. I went there the other day, and no one suspecting that I was a political correspondent, I was admitted without difficulty to view the gigantic arsenal and its 5,000,000 warriors. The poor workman out of whose head the fully-armed tin-soldiers sprang—*viâ* the sardine box—is now a rich man, and, what is more, an eager and keen-sighted patriot, who in his sphere has deserved well of his country. After retreating for years the French tin-soldiers once more advance; the German spiked-helmets retire every Christmas from the conquered positions in French nurseries, and maybe the time is not far off when the tricolour will wave over the toy shops of Berlin—a small revenge in awaiting the great one.

Many years have elapsed since the enemy placed his heel upon the neck of fallen France, but still to-day Paris is the metropolis of culture. Competition has led the *Article de Paris* to a commercial Sedan, and from a financial point of view, *le jouet Parisien* no longer belongs to the great powers of the toy-world. But the Paris doll will never admit the superiority of her German rival; she bears the stamp of nobility on her brow, and she means to rule the doll-world as before by right of her un-disputed rank and her artistic refinement. It surely needs very little human knowledge to distinguish her at once, the graceful Parisienne with her co-quettish smile, from one of the dull beauties of

Nuremberg or Hamburg. Should any hesitation be
possible a glance at her feet will suffice—the Parisienne's foot is small and dainty, and she is always
shod with a certain elegance, whilst Gretchen is
characteristically careless of her *chaussure*—just
as with us, for the matter of that. As for the rest
of her wardrobe, Germany, in spite of her war
indemnity of five milliards, is incapable of producing a tasteful doll-toilet; the delicate fingers of a
Paris *grisette* are required for this. It is therefore
considered the proper thing among German dolls
of fashion to import their dresses from some doll-
Worth in Paris. I can even tell you *entre nous* that
the really distinguished German dolls not only send
to Paris for their dresses but also for their heads.
The German doll manufacturers, incapable themselves of producing pretty and expressive doll
faces, buy their dolls' heads by retail from the
porcelain factories of Montreux and St. Maurice,
where they are modelled by first-rate artists, such
as a Carrier-Belleuse and others.

Up till now I have confined myself to the upper
classes of doll society, but even amongst the well-to-
do middle-class dolls of ten to fifteen francs apiece,
the difference between German and French is pal-
pable at first sight. The further one descends into
the lower regions of society, in the doll *bourgeoisie,*
the less clear becomes the national type. I will
undertake, however, to recognise my French friend

even amongst dolls of five francs apiece. To deter-
mine the nationality of a one-franc doll, it is necessary to possess great preliminary knowledge and
much natural aptitude. For the benefit of future
explorers in these still obscure regions of anthro-
pology, I may here point out an important item in
the necessary physical examination—the doll must
be shaken. If there is a rattling inside she is probably French, for the Paris *grisettes* who make these
dolls have a habit of putting some pebbles inside
them, which, I am told, tends to develop the taste
for vivisection amongst the rising generation.

Lower down in the series where the transition
type of Darwin is found, where the doll is without
either arms or legs, and where every trace of soul
has vanished from her impassive wooden face,
stamped with the same passionless calm which
characterises the marble folk of antiquity, or where
an unconscious smile alone glides over the rudi-
mentary features into which the pulp has hardened,
where the nose is nothing but a prophetic outline,
and where the black eyes are still shaded by the
chaotic darkness out of which the first doll rose—
there all national distinctions cease, there the em-
bryo doll lives her life of Arcadian simplicity,
undisturbed by all political agitations in the land
which gave her birth; the doll *à treize sous* does not
emigrate, maybe from patriotic motives, maybe

from lack of initiative.[1] Her rôle in life is humble; she belongs to the despised. Her place in the large toyshops is in a dark corner behind the other dolls, who stretch forth their jointed arms towards better-to-do purchasers, and with gleaming glass eyes and laughing lips appropriate the admiring glances of all the customers. But far away in the deserted streets of the suburbs, where the whole toyshop consists of a portable table and the public of a crowd of ragged urchins—there the doll *à treize sous* reigns supreme. By the flickering light of the lantern illuminating the modest fairy-world which Christmas and the New Year reveals to the children of the poor, there the despised doll becomes as beautiful as a queen and is surrounded by her whole court of admirers.

And I myself am one of her admirers. None of the fashionable beauties of the Magasin du Louvre has ever made my heart beat one whit the faster; none of the charming coquettes of the Bon Marché has succeeded in catching me in the net of her blond tresses; but I admit the tender sympathy with which my eyes rest upon the coarse features of the doll *à treize sous*. Everyone to his taste—I think

[1] The doll *à treize sous* is a characteristic Parisian type; she belongs to the family of *poupards*, and is usually made of *papier-mâché* or wood. After the making of the head the creative power of the artist comes to a sudden standstill; the rest of the body is only a sketch, and loses itself in an oblong chaos.

she is handsome; I cannot help it. And we have often met; chance leads me frequently across her path. But fancy if it were not chance! fancy if it were instead my undeclared affection which so often guided my steps to these places where I knew I should meet my sweetheart! fancy if I were falling in love at last! At all events I haven't said anything to her, nor has she ever said a word to me either of encouragement or rebuff. But, as I said before, we often meet at the houses of mutual friends, and sometimes, especially at Christmas and New Year, have we come together there. My visit does not impress them very much, but what happiness does not the doll spread around her! Realising my subordinate rôle, I willingly bow before the superior social talents of my companion, and silently in a corner by myself I enjoy her success. I don't know how she manages it, but she has hardly crossed the threshold before it seems to grow brighter inside the dark garret where live the children of the poor. The light radiates from the sparkling eyes of the little ones, glimmers in a faint smile on the pale cheek of the sick brother, and falls like a halo round the bald head of the doll. The little fellow crawling on the floor suddenly ceases his sobbing; he forgets that he is cold, he forgets that he is hungry, and with radiant joy he stretches out his arms to welcome the unexpected guest. And later at night, when it is time for me to go away, when the children of the rich have danced themselves tired round the Christmas tree, when the soldier's bugle has sounded in the boys' nursery, and when the little girls' smart dolls have been put to sleep each in her dainty bed—then little sister up in the garret tenderly wraps mother's ragged shawl round her beloved doll, for the night is cold and the doll has nothing on; and so they fall asleep side by side together, the doll *à treize sous* and her grateful little admirer.

Despised and ridiculed by us grown-up people, whose eyes have been led astray by the modern demand for realism, it is nevertheless a fact, that the doll *à treize sous* in the freshness of her primitive naïvety approaches nearer the ideal than the costly beauties of the Louvre and Bon Marché, who have reached the highest summit of refinement. We grown-up people have lost the faculty of understanding this from the moment we lost the simplicity of our childhood, but our teacher in this, as in many other things, is the little chap who still crawls about on the floor. Put a smart doll of fashion side by side with a simple pauper doll whose shape is as yet barely human, and you will see that the child usually stretches out his arms towards the latter. It sounds like a paradox, but it is a fact that you can easily verify for yourself; these cheap toys are, as a rule, preferred even by the children of the rich—that is to say, as long as they are real children and unconscious of the value of money. Later on, when they have acquired this knowledge, they are driven out from the Eden of childhood, their eyes are opened to the nakedness of the pauper doll, and what I have just said ceases to be true.

But the "political agitations"—what has become of them? Far away from all political storms and quarrels, my thoughts have fled to the garret idyll of the pauper doll; I have tried to sketch her as she has so often revealed herself to me; I have lifted a corner of the veil of unmerited oblivion which conceals her humble existence, there where she lives to bring joy to those whom the world rears to sorrow. I have done so as a tribute of gratitude for the pure joy which she has so often given me also, although I am myself too old to play with dolls. But, thank God, I am not too old to look on!

The doll is not old, and old age will never touch her—she will never grow old; she dies young, even as the hero, beloved of the gods. She dies young, and the first few weeks of the New Year have hardly passed away before she wends her way to the strange Elysian fields, where all that survives of broken toys sleeps under the shade of withered Christmas trees.

CHAPTER III

MONSIEUR ALFREDO

III

MONSIEUR ALFREDO

I DO not in the least know how I happened to come
upon the modest little café, nor do I know how it
came to pass that during the whole of that year I
frequented no other.

I wonder whether it was not on account of Monsieur Alfredo that I became an *habitué* there.

He evidently had his luncheon later than I, as
I had already had time to smoke a couple of
cigarettes before he made his appearance at the
Café de l'Empereur, upright and trim in his tightly
buttoned frock-coat, a roll of manuscript under his
arm, and his grey hair in neat curls surrounding
his wrinkled, childlike face. The waiter brought
him his little cup of coffee, and placed the chess-
board between us. Monsieur Alfredo, with old-
fashioned courtesy, inquired after my health, and
I on my side received satisfactory assurances as to
his well-being. I busied myself in placing the chess-
men, and whilst I groped under the table to find
that pawn which somehow or other had always
fallen to the ground, Monsieur Alfredo rapidly

produced his lump of sugar out of his pocket and put it into his cup.

We always played two games. I am singularly unlucky in games, and the old man, who loved chess, beamed all over every time he checkmated me. He played very slowly, but with amazing boldness, and even after having played with him every day for months together, I was still incapable of forming an opinion as to which of us played the worse. What puzzled me most of all was the fact that Monsieur Alfredo seldom or never played anything but kings and queens; occasionally, with reluctance, he would put the knights, castles, and bishops into requisition, but as to the pawns, he appeared to ignore them altogether. I had never before seen anybody play in this way, and often enough I had to look very sharp to make sure of losing.

The conversation turned on literature, and above all, the theatre. Monsieur Alfredo was extremely exacting as to dramatic art, and approved of no other form than the tragic. He was exceedingly difficult as to authors. I was just then full of Victor Hugo, but Monsieur Alfredo considered him much too sentimental. Racine and Corneille he thought better of, although he gave me to understand he considered them lacking in power. He despised comedy, and refused point-blank to admit Scribe, Augier, Labiche, or Dumas as celebrities. One only

needed to mention the name of Offenbach or Lecocq
to make the otherwise peaceful Monsieur Alfredo
quite furious; he then burst forth in Italian, which
he never spoke unless greatly excited; he denounced
them as "Birbanti," and "Avvelenatori," [1]—they
had with their music spread the poison which had
killed the good taste of a whole generation, and
they were, to a great extent, responsible for the
downfall of tragedy in our days.

He seemed well informed in everything concern-
ing the Paris theatres, and was evidently a frequent
playgoer himself. I had once or twice hinted that
we should go to the theatre together some evening,
but had noticed that Monsieur Alfredo never
seemed willing to understand me. As soon as we
had finished our second game, Monsieur Alfredo
produced four sous wrapped up in paper, called
the waiter, and asked what he had to pay, and laid
his four sous on the table. The Café de l'Empereur
was not a very expensive place, as you may per-
ceive; on the Boulevard St. Michel they charged
you eight sous for a cup of coffee, here you only
had to pay four if you took it without milk or
sugar—Monsieur Alfredo had long ago confided
to me his experience that sugar took away half the
fragrance of coffee. Not being so particular, I had
both sugar and milk with my coffee, and cognac
besides, but never once had I succeeded in getting

[1] Scoundrels and poisoners.

Monsieur Alfredo to accept *un petit verre* from me. I had tried to tempt him with everything the Café de l'Empereur could offer, but the old gentleman had always declined courteously but firmly.

I knew that Monsieur Alfredo was an author, and that it was the manuscript of a five-act tragedy he carried under his arm. I have always admired authors and artists, and I tried my best to make him understand how flattered I felt by his society. I had long ago told him everything about myself and my affairs, but Monsieur Alfredo displayed a singular reticence in all that concerned himself. Sometimes on leaving the café together I had tried to accompany him for a while, but, once in the streets, he always wished me good-bye, and I could easily see that I was not wanted. I had also expressed a wish to be allowed to call upon him, but had been given to understand that his time was very limited just then, and feeling sure that the tragedy was the cause of it all, I took good care not to disturb him.

He never came to the café in the evening, so I then lounged there alone smoking. Every now and then I dined with some of my fellow-students down on the boulevards, but as true inhabitants of the Quartier Latin, it was only seldom that we crossed the Seine. One evening, however, someone at the dinner-table proposed that we should all drive down to the Variétés to see Offenbach's "Les Brigands," which was the rage just then, and somehow or another they carried me off with them.

I believe the whole pit was full of students. We were in tremendous spirits, and applauded quite as vigorously as the *claque* which occupied the row behind us. It seemed to me as though I were playing my old friend from the Café de l'Empereur false, and I felt how he would despise me had he seen me in such a place, and I made up my mind not to tell him anything about it. But I could not help it, I roared with laughter the whole time. The last words of a song were hardly over before the *claque* broke out with deafening applause, and we and the whole pit followed their lead with right good will. And so when we collapsed and could move our arms no longer, the *claque* had recuperated its strength, and the brilliant farce was hailed once more with thundering applause by the joyless spectators behind us, where a whole chorus of poor devils shouted "bravo, bravo!" for their next day's bread.

Suddenly I was startled by a "bravo, bravo!" which came a little after the rest. I turned rapidly round, and ran my eye over the *claque,* and then, to the astonishment of my comrades, I took my hat and slunk out of the theatre.

The joyous music rang in my ears the whole way home, but I felt that tears were not far from my eyes that night.

No, I never told Monsieur Alfredo that I had
been to see "Les Brigands." I never alluded again
in our conversations to Offenbach and Lecocq, and
never more did I try to accompany the old gentleman to the theatre.

Next day, after we had finished our game at
chess, I followed him home at some little distance.
I went to his house that same evening, and whilst
I stood there contemplating the card on Monsieur
Alfredo's door, the *concierge* made her appearance,
and informed me that he never spent the evenings
at home. "Was I perhaps a pupil?" I answered in
the affirmative. I asked her if he had many pupils
just then, and she answered I was the first she had
ever seen.

It was towards the end of autumn that I communicated to Monsieur Alfredo my irrevocable
decision to throw medicine to the winds and to
devote myself to the stage, and to my great satisfaction he consented to become my instructor in
deportment and declamation. The lessons were
given in my rooms in the Hôtel de l'Avenir. The
old fellow's method was a peculiar one, and his
theories on acting as bold as those he held on
chess. I listened with the utmost attention to all
he said, and tried as well as I could to learn the
fundamental rules of deportment he saw fit to
teach me. After a while he acceded to my request
to be allowed to try myself in a rôle, and fully

aware of my preference for tragedy, it was decided
that under the immediate superintendence of the
author himself, I should get up one of the
characters in Monsieur Alfredo's last work, "Le
Poignard," a tragedy in five acts. Monsieur Alfredo himself was the king and I was the marquis.
I admit that my *début* was not a happy one. I saw
that the author was far from satisfied with me, and
I realised that my marquis was a dead failure. My
next *début* was in the rôle of the English lord in
the five-act tragedy, "La Vengeance," but neither
there were there any illusions possible as to the
result. I then tried my luck as the count in "Le
secret du Tombeau," but with a very doubtful issue.
I then sank down to a viscount, and made super-
human efforts to keep up to the mark, but notwithstanding the indulgent way in which Monsieur
Alfredo pointed out my shortcomings, I could not
conceal from myself the fact that I was not fit to
be a viscount either.

I began to have serious doubts as to my theatrical
vocation, but Monsieur Alfredo thought that the
reason of my failure might be traced to my un-
familiarity with the highest society, and my difficulty in adapting myself to the sensations and
thoughts of these high personages. And he was
right—it was anything but easy. All his heroes and
heroines were very sorry for themselves, not to say
desperate, although as a rule it was impossible for

me to understand the reason of their being so. Love
and hatred glowed in everyone's eyes. True that
as a rule everything went wrong for the lovers, but
even if they got each other at last, they did not
seem to be a bit the more cheerful for that. I remember, for instance, the third act of "Le Poignard," where I (the marquis), after having waded
through blood, succeed in winning the lady of my
heart, who on her side has gone through fire and
water to be mine. The archbishop marries us by
moonlight, and we, who had not seen each other
for ten years, are left alone for a while in a bower
of roses. We had nothing on earth to be afraid of;
no one was likely to disturb us, as I had previously
run my sword through every grown-up person in
the play, and I thought that I ought to be a little
kind to the marchioness. But Monsieur Alfredo
never found my voice tragic enough during the few
brief moments of happiness he granted us. (We
perished shortly afterwards in an earthquake.)

For the matter of that, those who escaped a
violent death were not much better off—they were
carried away in any case in the flower of their
youth by sudden inexplicable ailments, which no
amount of care could contend against. At first I
tried to save some of the victims, but Monsieur
Alfredo always looked very astonished when I sug-
gested that someone might be allowed to recover;
and knowing his theory that it was sentimentality

that spoiled Victor Hugo as a dramatist, I ceased more and more to interfere in the matter.

After a few more abortive attempts to pose as a nobleman, I submitted to Monsieur Alfredo my opinion that I might do better in a more humble position. But here we were met by an unforeseen obstacle—Monsieur Alfredo did not descend below viscounts. If by the exigencies of the plot a lonely representative of the lower orders had to appear on the scene, he had no sooner got a word out of his mouth before the author would fling a purse at his head, and send him back into the wings with an imperial wave of his shiny coat sleeve. Well, away with all false pride! It was in these rôles I at last hit upon my true *genre;* it was here I scored my only triumphs. Imperceptibly to the old man, I disappeared more and more from the *répertoire,* would now and then cross the stage and with a deep obeisance deliver a manuscript letter from some crowned head, or would occasionally come to carry off a corpse—that was all.

So the autumn passed on, we had gone through one tragedy after another, and still Monsieur Alfredo constantly turned up with a new manuscript under his arm. I began to be afraid that the old man would wear himself out with this fathomless authorship, and I tried in every possible way to make him rest a little. This was, however, quite impossible. He now came every single day to Hôtel de l'Avenir to his only pupil and literary confidant. His guileless, childish face seemed to grow more and more gentle, and more and more was I drawn towards the poor old enthusiast with a sort of tender sympathy.

And unquenchable and ever more unquenchable became his literary bloodthirstiness. By Christmastime his new tragedy was ready, and Monsieur Alfredo himself looked upon it as his best work. The scene was laid in Sicily at the foot of Mount Etna in the midst of burning lava-streams. Not a soul survived the fifth act. I begged for the life of a Newfoundland dog, who, with a dead heir in his mouth, had swam over from the mainland, but Monsieur Alfredo was inexorable. The dog threw himself into the crater of Etna in the last scene.

But while the lava of Mount Etna was heating Monsieur Alfredo's dream-world, the winter snow was falling over Paris. All of us had long since taken to our winter coats, but my poor professor was still wandering about in his same old frockcoat, so shiny with constant brushing, so threadbare with the wear and tear of years. The nights became so cold, and sadly did I follow in my thoughts the poor old man tramping home from the Variétés every night. Many times was I very near broaching the delicate subject, but was always deterred by the sensitive pride with which he sought to disguise his poverty. Yet had I never seen him in such excellent spirits as he was just then; he placed greater expectations than ever on his new tragedy. Like all his previous plays it was written for the Théâtre Français. The systematic ill-will with which Mons. Perrin[1] had refused to accept any work of his had certainly made him turn his thoughts to the Odéon Theatre; but with due consideration to the colossal proportions of his new drama, Monsieur Alfredo did not quite see his way to avoid offering it to the very first theatre in Paris.

Maybe it seems to you that I ought to have pointed out to Monsieur Alfredo the dangerous flights of his imagination, that I ought to have tried to make him realise that his theatre was erected on quite another planet than ours. I did nothing of the sort, and you would not have done so either had you known him as I did, had you witnessed the anxiety with which his kind eyes sought for my approval, how his sad old child-face brightened up when he recited some passage which he expected would especially dumbfound me—which, alas! it seldom failed to do. I had come so far that I was quite incapable of spoiling his pleasure by a single word of criticism. Silently I listened to tragedy after tragedy, and there was no need to simulate being serious, for all my laughter over his wild creations was silenced by the tragedy of reality, all my criticism was disarmed by his utter helplessness—

[1] The then manager of the Théâtre Français.

he did not even possess an overcoat! The only audience the poor old man ever had was me, why then shouldn't I applaud him a little, he whom life had so unmercifully hissed?

One afternoon he did not turn up at the Café de l'Empereur, and in vain I waited for him before the chess-board the next day. I waited still another day, but then, driven by uneasy forebodings, I went to look him up towards evening. The *concierge* had not seen him go out, and there was no answer to my knock at his door. I stood there for a moment or two looking at the faded old visiting-card nailed on his door—

> Mr. *ALFREDO*
>
> *Auteur Dramatique, Professeur de Déclamation, de Maintien et de Mise en Scène.*

And then I quietly opened the door and went in.

The old man lay on his bed delirious, not recognising the unbidden guest who stood there, sadly looking round the empty garret, cold as the streets without, for there was not even a fireplace.

It was sunny and bright next day, and it was easy to remove him to the hospital close by—I was on the staff there for the matter of that. He had pneumonia. They were all very kind to the old gentleman, both the doctors and the students, and dear Sœur Philomène managed matters so successfully that she got a private room for him. He continued delirious the whole of that day and night, but towards morning he became conscious and recognised me. He then insisted on returning at once to his own quarters, but quieted down considerably on being told he was in a private room, and that he was quite independent of all the other patients. After some hesitation he inquired what he would have to pay, and I answered him I did not think the hospital could charge him anything, as the "Société des Auteurs Dramatiques" was entitled to a free bed, and I doubted whether it would be the right thing to refuse to avail himself of this privilege, as of course every one knew who he was. Sœur Philomène, who stood behind his pillow, shook her finger reprovingly at my little white lie, but I could well see by the expression of her eyes that she forgave me. I had touched the poor old author's most sensitive chord; with keenest interest he made me repeat over and over again what I had said about the "Société des Auteurs Dramatiques," and a faint smile of contentment lit up his faded old face when at last I had succeeded in making him believe me. From that moment he seemed quite pleased and satisfied with everything, and he did not realise himself how rapidly he was sinking.

According to his wish, a little table with writing materials had been placed beside his bed, but he had not yet tried to write anything.

The night had been worse than usual, and during the morning round I noticed that Sœur Philomène had hung a little crucifix at the head of his bed. He lay there quite silent the whole day; once only when he was given his broth he asked for the name of the most deadly poison on record, and Sœur Philomène thought it was prussic acid.

Towards evening he became more feverish, and his eyes began to be restless. He begged me to sit down beside him, and after swearing me over to secrecy he unveiled to me the plot of his new tragedy where the rival gives prussic acid to the bride and bridegroom during the wedding ceremony. He spoke rapidly and cheerfully, and with a triumphant glance he asked me whether I thought the Théâtre Français would dare to reject his play this time, and I answered that I did not believe it would dare to do so. The work was to proceed with great speed, the first act was to be ready next morning, and in a week's time at the very latest he intended to send in the manuscript for perusal.

He became more and more delirious, and he did not pay any attention to my answers. His eye still rested on mine, but his horizon widened more and more, for the barriers of this world began to fall away. His speech became more and more incoherent, and I could no longer follow his staggering thought. But his face still expressed what his failing perception could no longer form into words, and in silent wonder I witnessed death bestow on him the joy that life had denied him.

He seemed to listen. A light passed over his pale face, his eyes sparkled, and with head erect the old man sat up in bed. He shook away his grey curls, and a shimmer of triumph fell over his brow. With his hand on his heart the dying author made a low bow, for in the silence of the falling night he heard the echo of his life's fondest dream; he heard the Théâtre Français ringing with applause!

And slowly the curtain sank upon the old author's last tragedy.

CHAPTER IV

ITALY IN PARIS

Italy in Paris

AT ONE time I had many patients in the Roussel
Yard. Ten or twelve families lived there, but none
were so badly off, I believe, as the Salvatore
family. At Salvatore's it was so dark that they
were obliged to burn a little oil-lamp the whole day,
and there was no fireplace except a brazier which
stood in the middle of the room. Damp as a cellar
it was at all times; but when it rained the water
penetrated into the room, which lay a couple of feet
lower than the street.

And, nevertheless, one could see in everything a
kind of pathetic struggle against the gloomy impression which pervaded the whole dwelling. Old
illustrated papers were pasted up round the walls,
the bed was neat and clean, and behind an old curtain in one corner, the family's little wardrobe was
hung up in the neatest order. Salvatore himself,
with skilful hands, had made the little girls' bed out
of an old box, and in the day one could sit upon it
as if it were a sofa. The corner shelf where the
Madonna stood was adorned with bright-coloured
paper flowers, and there the small treasures of the

family lay spread out—the gilt brooch which Salvatore had presented to his wife when they were married; the string of corals which her brother had brought from the coral fishery in "Barbaria" (Algeria); the two gorgeous cups out of which coffee was drunk on solemn occasions; and there, too, stood the wonderful porcelain dog which Concetta had once received as a present from a grand lady, and which was only taken down on Sundays to be admired more closely.

I never understood how the mother managed it; but the little girls were always neat and tidy in their outgrown clothes, and their faces shone, so washed and scrubbed were they. The eldest child, Concetta, had been at the free school for more than half a year; and it was the mother's pride to make her read aloud to me out of her book. She herself had never learned to read, and although I allowed myself to be told that Salvatore read very well, neither he nor I had ever ventured to put his capabilities in that direction to the test. Now since Petruccio could hardly ever get out of bed, Concetta had been obliged to give up going to school, so that she might stay at home with her sick brother, whilst *la mamma* was at her work away in the pothouse. This job could not be given up, as not only did she get ten sous a day for washing dishes, but sometimes she could bring home scraps under her apron, which no one else could turn to account, but out of which she managed to make a capital soup for Petruccio.

Salvatore himself worked the whole day away in La Villette. He was obliged to be at the stone-mason's yard at six o'clock every morning, and it was much too far to go home during mid-day rest. Sometimes it happened that I was there when he came home in the evening after his day's work, and then he looked very proudly at me when Petruccio stretched out his arms towards him. He took his little son up so carefully with his big horny hands, lifted him on his broad shoulders, and tenderly leaned his sun-burnt cheek against the sick little one's waxen face. Petruccio sat quite quiet and silent on his father's arm; sometimes he laid hold of his father's matted beard with his thin fingers, and then Salvatore looked very happy. "Vedete, Signor dottore," he then would say, "n'è vero che sta meglio sta sera?" [1] He received his week's wages every Saturday, and then he often came home triumphantly with a little toy for his son, and both father and mother knelt down beside the bed to see how Petruccio liked it. Petruccio, alas! scarcely liked anything. He took the toy in his hand, but that was all. Petruccio's face was old and withered, and his solemn, weary eyes were not the eyes of a child. I had never known him to cry or complain, but neither had I seen him smile except once when

[1] "Is it not true that he is better to-night?"

he was given a great hairy horse—a horse which stretched out its tongue when one turned it upside down. But it was not every day that a horse like that could be found.

Petruccio was six years old, but he could not speak. He would lie hour after hour quite quiet and silent, but he did not sleep: his great eyes stood wide open, and it seemed as if he saw something far beyond the narrow walls of the room—"Sta sempre in pensiero," [1] said Salvatore. Petruccio was supposed to understand everything which was said around him, and nothing of importance was undertaken in the little family without first trying to discover Petruccio's opinion on the subject; and if any one believed that they could read disapproval in the features of the soulless little one, the whole question fell to the ground at once, and it was afterwards found that Petruccio had almost always been right.

On Sundays Salvatore sat at home, and there were usually some other holiday-dressed workmen visiting him, and in low-toned voices they sat and argued about wages, about news from *il paese,* and sometimes Salvatore treated them to a litre of wine, and they played a game, *alla scopa.* Sometimes it was supposed that Petruccio wished to look on, and then his little bed was moved to the bench where they sat; and sometimes Petruccio wished to be

---

[1] "He lies always buried in thought."

alone, and then Salvatore and his guests moved out into the passage. I had, however, noticed that Petruccio's wish to be alone, and the consequent removal of the company to the passage usually happened when the wife was away: if she were at home she saw plainly that Petruccio wished his father to stay indoors and not go out with the others. And Petruccio was right enough there too. Salvatore was not very difficult to persuade if one of the guests wished to treat him in his turn. Once out in the passage, it happened often enough that he went off to the public-house too. And once there, it was not so easy for Salvatore to get away again.

What was still more difficult was the coming home. His wife forgave him certainly—she had done it so many times before; but Salvatore knew that Petruccio was inexorable, and the thicker the mist of intoxication fell over him, the more crushed did he feel himself under Petruccio's reproachful eye. No dissimulation helped here; Petruccio saw through it at once. Petruccio could even see how much he had drunk, as Salvatore himself confided to me one Sunday evening when I came upon him sitting out in the passage, in the deepest repentance. Salvatore was, alas! obviously uncertain in his speech that evening, and it did not need Petruccio's perspicacity to see that he had drunk more than usual. I asked him if he would not go in, but he wished to remain outside to get *un poco d'aria;*

he was, however, very anxious to know if Petruccio were awake or not, and I promised to come out and tell him. I also thought it was best he should sit out there till his head should clear itself a little bit, though not so much for Petruccio's sake as to spare his wife; and for that matter this was not the first time I had been Salvatore's confidant in the like difficult situation. Those who watch the lives of the poor closely cannot be very severe upon a working man who, after he has toiled twelve hours a day the whole week, sometimes gets a little wine into his head. It is a melancholy fact, but we must judge it leniently; for we must not forget that here at least society has hardly offered the poorer classes any other distraction.

I therefore advised my friend Salvatore to sit outside till I came back, and I went in alone. Inside sat the wife with her child of sorrow in her arms; and the even breathing of the little girls could be heard from the box. Petruccio was supposed to know me very well, and even to be fond of me although he had never shown it in any way, nor, as far as I knew, had any feeling whatsoever been mirrored in his face. The mother's eye, so clear-sighted in everything, was nevertheless unable to see that there was no soul in the child's vacant eye; the mother's ear, so sensitive to each breath of the little one, yet failed to hear that the confused sounds which sometimes came from his lips would never form themselves into human language. Petruccio had been ill from his birth, his body was shrunken, and no thought lived under the child's wrinkled forehead. Unhappily I could do nothing for him; all I could hope for was that the ill-favoured little one would soon die. And it looked as if his release were near. That Petruccio had been worse for some time both the mother and I had understood; and this evening he was so feeble that he was not able to hold his head up. Petruccio had refused all food since yesterday, and Salvatore's wife, when I came in, was just trying to persuade him, with all the sweet words which only a mother knows, to swallow a little milk; but he would not. In vain the mother put the spoon to his mouth and said that it was wonderfully good, in vain did she appeal to my presence, "Per fare piacere al Signor dottore," [1]— Petruccio would not. His forehead was puckered, and his eyes had a look of painful anxiety, but no complaint came from his tightly compressed lips.

Suddenly the mother gave a scream. Petruccio's face was distorted with cramp, and a strong convulsion shook his whole little body. The attack was soon over; and whilst Petruccio was being laid in his bed, I tried to calm the mother as well as I could by telling her that children often had convulsions

[1] "To please the doctor."

which were of very little importance, and that there was no further danger from this one now. I looked up and my eye fell upon Salvatore, who stood leaning against the door-post. He had taken courage and had staggered to the door, and, unseen by us, he had witnessed that sight so terrifying to unaccustomed eyes. He was as pale as a corpse, and great tears ran down the cheeks which a moment before were flushed with drink. "Castigo di Dio! Castigo di Dio!" [1] muttered he with trembling voice; and he fell on his knees by the door, as if he dared not approach the feeble cripple who seemed to him like God's mighty avenger.

The unconscious little son had once more shown his father the right way; Salvatore went no more to the public-house.

Petruccio grew worse and worse, and the mother no longer left his side. And it was scarcely a month after she lost her place that Salvatore's accident happened; he fell from a scaffolding and broke his leg. He was taken to the Lariboisière Hospital; and the company for whom he worked paid fifty centimes a day to his family, which they were not obliged to do, so that Salvatore's wife had to be very grateful for it. Every Thursday—the visiting day at the hospital—she was with him for an hour; and I too saw him now and then. The days went on, and Petruccio's home grew more and more

[1] "The punishment of God."

destitute. The porcelain dog now stood alone on
the Madonna's shelf; and it was not long before the
holiday clothes went the same way as the treasures
—to the pawn-shop. Petruccio needed broth and
milk every day, and he had them. The little girls
too had enough, I believe, to still their hunger more
or less; but what the mother herself lived upon I
do not know.

I had already tried many times to take Petruccio
to the children's hospital, where he would have been
much better off, but as usual all my powers of elo-
quence could not achieve this: the poor, as is well
known, will hardly ever be separated from their
sick children. The lower middle class and the town
artisans have learnt to understand the value of the
hospital, but the really poor mother, whose culture
is very low, will not leave the side of her sick child:
the exceptions to this rule are very rare.

And so came the 15th, the dreaded day when the
quarter's rent must be paid, when the working man
drags his mattress to the pawn-shop and the wife
draws off her ring, which in her class means much
more than in ours; the day full of terror, when
numberless suppliants stand with lowered heads
before their landlord, and when hundreds of families do not know where they will sleep the next
night.

I happened to pass by there on that very evening and at the door stood Salvatore's little girl

crying all by herself. I asked her why she cried, but that she did not know; at last, however, I got out of her that she cried because "la mamma piange tanto."[1] Inside the yard I ran against my friend Archangelo Fusco, the street-sweeper, who lived next door to the Salvatores. He was busy dragging his bed out into the yard, and I did not need to wait for his explanation to understand that he had been evicted.[2] I asked him where he was going to move to, and he hoped to sleep that night at the Refuge in the Rue Tocqueville, and afterwards he meant to find some other place. Inside sat Salvatore's wife crying by Petruccio's bed, and on the table stood a bundle containing the clothes of the family. The Salvatore family had not been able to pay their rent, and the Salvatore family had been evicted. The landlord had been there that afternoon, and had said that the room was let from the morning of the next day. I asked her where she thought of going, and she said she did not know.

I had often heard the dreaded landlord talked of; the year before I had witnessed the same sorrowful scene, when he had turned out into the street a couple of unhappy families and laid hands upon the little they possessed. I had never seen him personally, but I thought it might be useful in my study of human nature to make his acquaintance.

[1] "Mamma cries so."

[2] The landlord can take everything in such cases except the bed and the clothes.

Archangelo Fusco offered to take me to him, and
we set forth slowly. On the way my companion
informed me that the landlord was *molto ricco;* besides the whole court he owned a large house in
the vicinity, and this did not surprise me in the
least, because I had long known that he secretly
carried on that most lucrative of all professions,
money-lending to the poor. Archangelo Fusco considered that he on his side had nothing to gain by
a meeting with the landlord, and after he had told
me that besides the rent he also owed him ten francs,
we agreed that he should only accompany me to the
entrance.

A shabbily dressed old man, with a bloated, dis-
agreeable face opened the door carefully, and after
he had looked me over, admitted me into the room.
I mentioned my errand, and asked him to allow
Salvatore to settle his rent in a few days' time. I
told him that Salvatore himself lay in the hospital,
that the child was dying, and that his severity towards these poor people was inhuman cruelty. He
asked who I was, and I answered that I was a
friend of the family. He looked at me, and with an
ugly laugh he said that I could best show that by
at once paying their rent. I felt the blood rushing
to my head, I hope and believe it was only with
anger, for one never need be ashamed of not being
rich. I listened for a couple of minutes whilst he
abused my poor destitute Italians with the coarsest

words; he said that they were a dirty thieving pack, who did not deserve to be treated like human beings; that Salvatore drank up his wages; that the street-sweeper had stolen ten francs from him; and that they all of them well deserved the misery in which they lived.

I asked if he needed this money just now, and from his answer I understood that no prayers would avail here. He was rich; he owned over 50,000 francs in money, he said, and he had begun with nothing of his own. It is a melancholy fact that the man who has risen from destitution to riches is usually cruel to the poor: one would hope and believe the contrary, but this is unhappily the case.

My intention when I went there had been to endeavour diplomatically to come to some sort of agreement, but alas! I was not the man for that. I lost my temper altogether, and went further than I had intended to do, as usual. At first he answered me scornfully and with coarse insults, but he gradually grew silent, and I ended by talking alone I should say for nearly half an hour's time. It would serve no purpose to relate what I said to him; there are occasions when it is legitimate to show one's anger in action, but it is always a mistake to show it in words. I said to him, however, that this money which had been squeezed out of the poor was the wages of sin; that his debt to all these poor human

beings was far greater than theirs to him. I pointed
to the crucifix which hung against the wall, and I
said that if any divine justice was to be found on
this earth, vengeance could not fail to reach him,
and that no prayers could buy his deliverance from
the punishment that awaited him, for his life was
stained with the greatest of all sins—namely,
cruelty towards the poor. "And take care, old
blood-sucker!" I shouted out at last in a threatening voice; "you owe your money to the poor, but
you owe yourself to the devil, and the hour is at
hand when he will demand his own again!" I
checked myself, startled, for the man sank down
in his chair as if touched by an invisible hand, and
pale as death, he stared at me with a terror which
I felt communicated itself to me. The curse I had
just called down still rang in my ears with a strange
uncanny sound which I did not recognise; and it
seemed to me as if there were some one else in the
room besides us two.

I was so agitated that I have no recollection of
how I came away. When I got home it was already
late, but I did not sleep a wink all night; and even
to this day I think with wonder of the waking
dream which that night filled me with an inconceiv-
able horror. I dreamt that I had condemned a man
to death.

When I got there in the forenoon the blow had

already fallen upon me. I knew what had happened
although no human being had told me. All the
inhabitants of the yard were assembled before the
door in eager talk. "Sapete Signor dottore?" [1] they
called out as soon as they saw me.

"Yes, I know," answered I, and hurried to Salvatore's. I bent down over Petruccio and pretended
to examine his chest; but breathless I listened to
every word that the wife said to me.

The landlord had come down there late yesterday
evening, she said. The little girl had run away and
hidden herself when he came into the room; but
Concetta had remained behind her mother's chair,
and when he asked why they were so afraid of him,
Concetta had answered because he was so cruel to
mamma. He had sat there upon the bench a long
time without saying a word, but he did not look
angry, Salvatore's wife thought. At last he said to
her she need not be anxious about the rent; she
could wait to pay it till next time. And when he
left he laid a five-franc piece upon the table to buy
something for Petruccio. Outside the door he had
met Archangelo Fusco with his bed on a hand-cart,
preparing to take himself off, and he had told the
street-sweeper too that he could remain in his lodg-
ing. He had asked Archangelo Fusco about me,
and Archangelo Fusco, who judged me with friendship's all-forgiving forbearance, had said nothing

[1] "Do you know, doctor?"

unkind about me. He had then gone on his way, and according to what was discovered by the police investigations he had, contrary to his habit, passed the evening at the public-house close by, and the porter had thought he looked drunk when he came home. As he lived quite alone, and for fear of thieves or from avarice, attended to his housekeeping himself, no one knew what had happened, but lights were burning in the house the whole night, and when he did not come down in the morning, and his door was fastened inside, they had begun to suspect foul play and sent for the police. He was still warm when they cut him down; but the doctor whom the police sent for said that he had already been dead a couple of hours. They had not been able to discover the smallest reason for his hanging himself. All that was known was that he had been visited in the evening by a strange gentleman who had stayed with him more than an hour, and the neighbours had heard a violent dispute going on inside. No one in the house had seen the strange gentleman before, and no one knew who he was.

. . . .

The Roussel Yard now belongs to the dead man's brother; and to my joy the new landlord's first action was to have the rooms in it repaired, so that now they look more habitable. He also lowered the rents.

The Salvatores moved thence when Petruccio died; but the place is still full of Italians. I go there now and then; and in spite of all the talk about the Paris doctors' *jalousie de métier,* I have never yet met any one who tried to oust me in this practice.

CHAPTER V

RAFFAELLA

V

RAFFAELLA

THE picture was considered one of the very best in the whole Salon, and the young painter's name was on every one's lips. It was always surrounded by a group of admirers, fascinated by its beauty. She lay there on a couch of purple, and around her loveliness there fell as it were a shimmer from life's May-sun. Refined art-critics had settled her age to be at most sixteen. There was still something of the enchanting grace of the child in her slender limbs, and it was as if a veil of innocence protected her.

Who was she, the fair-limbed maiden with the noble head? Was it true, what rumour whispered, that the original of the dazzling picture bore one of the greatest names of France, that a high-born beauty of the Faubourg St. Germain had, unknown to the man, allowed the artist to behold the ideal he had sought for but never found? Who was she?

The doctor had stood there for awhile listening to the murmur of praise which bore witness to the young painter's triumph, and slowly making his way through the fashionable crowd, he made for the exit. He stopped there for a moment or two watching one carriage after another roll down the

Champs Elysées, and then he wandered across the
Place de la Concorde and entered the Boulevard
St. Germain. The clock struck seven as he passed
St. Germain des Près, and he hastened his steps for
he still had a long way to go. He turned into one
of the small streets near the Jardin des Plantes,
and it soon seemed as if he had left Paris behind
him. The streets began to darken and narrowed
into lanes, the great shops shrank into small booths,
and the cafés became pot-houses. Fine coats became
more and more rare, and blouses more numerous.
It was nearly eight o'clock, just theatre time down
on the brilliant boulevards, and up here groups of
workmen wandered home after the day's toil. They
looked tired and heavy-hearted, but the work was
hard; at six in the morning already the bell rang in
the manufactories and workshops, and many of
them had an hour's walk to come there. Here and
there stood a ragged figure with outstretched hand,
he carried no inscription on his breast telling how
he became blind, he did not recite one word of the
story of his misery—he did not need to do that here,
for those that gave him a copper were poor themselves, and most of them had known what it meant
to be hungry.

The alleys became dirtier and dirtier, and heaps
of sweepings and refuse were left in the filthy gut-
ters; it did not matter so much up here, where only
poor people lived.

The doctor entered an old tumble-down house, and groped his way up the slippery dark stairs as high as he could go. An old woman met him at the door—he was expected. "Zitto, zitto!" (hush, hush), said the old woman, with her fingers on her lips; "she sleeps." And in a whisper *la nonna* (the grandmother) reported how things had been going on since yesterday. Raffaella had not been delirious in the night, she had lain quite still and calm the whole day, only now and then she had asked to see the child, and a short while ago she had fallen asleep with the little one in her arms. Did *il Signor dottore* wish to wake her? No, that he would not. He sat himself down in silence beside the old woman on the bench. They were very good friends these two, and he well knew the sad story of the family.

They were from St. Germano, the village up amongst the mountains half-way between Rome and Naples, whence most of the Italian models came. They had arrived in Paris barely two years ago with a number of men and women from their neighbourhood. Raffaella's mother had caught *la fabbre* and died at Hôtel Dieu a couple of months after their arrival, and the old woman and the grandchild had had to look after themselves alone in the foreign city.

And Raffaella had become a model, like so many others.

A young artist painted her picture. He painted her beautiful girlish head, he painted her young bosom. And then fell her poor clothes, and he painted her maiden loveliness in its budding spring, in the innocent peace of the sleeping senses. She was the butterfly-winged Psyche, whose lips Eros has not yet kissed; she was Diana's nymph who, tired after hunting, unfastens her chiton and, unseen by mortal eyes, bathes her maiden limbs in the hidden forest lake; she was the fair Dryad of the grove who falls asleep on her bed of flowers.

His last picture was ready. Fame entered the young artist's studio, and a ruined child went out from it.

They separated like good friends, he wrote down her address with a piece of charcoal on the wall, and she went to pose to another painter. So she went from studio to studio, and her innocence protected her no longer.

One day the old grandmother stood humbly at the door of the fashionable studio, and told between her sobs that Raffaella was about to become a mother. Ah, yes! he remembered her well, the beautiful girl, and he put some pieces of gold in the old woman's hand and promised to try to do something for her. And he kept his word. The same evening he proposed to his comrades to make a collection for Raffaella's child, and he assumed that there was no one who had the right to refuse. And there was no one who had the right to refuse. They all gave what they could, some more and some less, and more than one emptied his purse into the hat which went round for Raffaella's child. They all thought it was such a pity for her, the beautiful girl, to have had such bad luck. They wondered what would become of her, she might of course continue to be a model, but never would she be the same as before. The sculptors all agreed that the beautiful lines of the hip could never stand the trial, and the painters knew well that the exquisite delicacy of her colouring was lost for ever. The child would, of course, be put out to nurse in the country, and the money collected was enough to pay for a whole year. And it was not a bad idea either to beg their friend, that foreign doctor, who was so fond of Italians, to give an eye to Raffaella, he might perhaps be useful in many future contingencies.

And the doctor, who was so fond of Italians, had often been to see her of late. Raffaella had been so ill, so ill, she had been delirious for days and nights, and this was the first quiet sleep she had had for a long time.

No, the doctor certainly did not wish to wake her; he sat there in silence beside the old grandmother, deep in thought. He was thinking of Raffaella's story. It was not new to him, that story, the Italian poor quarter had more than once told it him, and he had often enough read it in books. It seemed to him that what he saw in life was far simpler and far sadder than what he read in books. Nor was there in Raffaella's story anything very unusual or very sensational, no great display of feeling either of sorrow or despair, no accusations, no threat for vengeance, no attempt at suicide. Everything had gone so simply in such everyday fashion. It was not with head erect and flaming eyes that the old grandmother had stood before him who was guilty of the child's fall, but in humble resignation she had stopped at the door and sobbed out their misery, and when she left she had prayed the Madonna to reward him for his charity. The poor old woman had her reasons for this—she could not carry her head erect, for life had long since bent her neck under the yoke of daily toil; her eyes could not flame with menace, for they had too often had to beg for bread. She knew not how to accuse, for she herself had been condemned unheard to oppression; she knew not how to demand justice, for life had meant for her one long endurance of wrongs. Her path had lain through darkness and misery, she had seen so little of life's sunlight, and her thoughts had grown so dim under her furrowed brow. She was dull, dull as an old worn-out beast of burden.

And the seducer, he was perhaps, after all, not more of a blackguard than many others. He had done what he could to atone for a fault which, from his point of view, was hardly to be considered so very great, he had provided for a whole year for a child which he said was none of his—what could he do more? He had asked the doctor if he knew of any virtuous models, and the doctor had answered him, "no," for neither did he know of any virtuous models.[1]

And Raffaella had borne her degradation as she had borne her poverty, without bitterness and without despair; she wept sometimes, but she accused no one, neither herself nor him who had injured her. She was resigned. Authors believe that it is so easy to jump into the Seine, or to take a dose of laudanum, but it is very difficult. Raffaella was a daughter of the people, no culture had entered into her thought-world, either with its light or its shadow, she was far too natural even to think of such a thing.

He who was educated had brought forward the question of sending the child into the country, or placing it in the *Enfants trouvés* (foundling hospital), and she who was uneducated had known of no other answer than to wind her arms still closer round her child's neck. And *la nonna* (the old grandmother) who scrubbed steps and carried coals

---

[1] I was for ten years the confidant, the friend, and the doctor to many of the poor Italians in Paris, the greater number of whom are models. My experience during these years was a terrible one. Nine years of Rome have made the evidence still more conclusive. Of English models I know nothing and have nothing to say.

all day, and having at last lulled the child to rest
in the evening, dead-tired went to sleep with half-
shut eyes and a string round her wrist, so as now
and then to rock the little one's cradle; neither
could she understand that it would be any relief if
la piccerella were to be sent away.

The light fell on the squalid bed, and the doctor
looked at his patient. Yes! it was indeed very like
her, he certainly was a clever artist that young
painter! Her face was only a little paler now, that
painful shadow over the forehead was probably not
to be seen in the bright studio where the picture
was painted, those dark rings round her eyes were
very likely not suitable for the *salon*. But the same
perfection in every feature, the same noble shape of
the head, the same childishly soft rounding of the
cheek, the same curly locks round the beautiful
brow. Yes, rumour spoke true, she bore the mark
of nobility on her forehead, not that of the Faubourg St. Germain, but that of Hellas, she bore
the features of the Venus of Milo.

It was quite still up there in the dim little garret.
The doctor watched the young mother who slept
so peacefully with her child in her arms, he watched
the old woman who sat by his side fingering her
rosary. With foreboding sadness he looked into the
future which awaited these three, and sorrowfully
his thoughts wandered along the way which lay
before his poor friends.

Ah yes, Raffaella soon got well, for she was healthy with Nature's youth. Model she never became again, for she could not leave her child. She did not marry, for her people do not forgive one who has had a child by a *signore*. With the baby at her breast she wandered about in search of work, any work. Her demands were so small, but her chances were still smaller. She found no work. The old woman still held out for a time, then she broke down, and Raffaella had to provide food for three mouths. The last savings were gone, and the Sunday clothes were at the pawn-shop. Public charity did not help her, for she was a foreigner, and private charity never came near Raffaella. She had to choose between destitution or going on the streets. Her child lived, and she chose destitution. Society did not reward her for her choice, for virtue hungers and freezes in the poor quarters of Paris. She ended, like so many others, by *fare la Scopa*.[1] Pale and emaciated sat the child on *la nonna's* knee, and with low bent back Raffaella swept the streets where pleasure and luxury went by. Poverty had effaced her beauty, she bore the features of want and hardship. Sorrow had furrowed her brow, but the stamp of nobility was still there. Hats off for virtue in rags! It is greater than the virtue of the Faubourg St. Germain!

[1] The harbour of refuge of many of the shipwrecked ones who still can and will work. The street scavengers of Paris are to a great extent Italians.

CHAPTER VI

MONT BLANC, KING OF THE MOUNTAINS

Mont Blanc,
King of the Mountains

"Mont Blanc is the monarch of mountains;
    They crowned him long ago
On a throne of rocks, in a robe of clouds,
    With a diadem of snow."

Byron.

Note.—This story may seem rather whimsical to any one unacquainted with a little adventure I had while descending Mont Blanc, an adventure which began in an avalanche and ended happily in a crevasse. The story dances away on the rope of a single metaphor, and dances over precipices. But I am still so under the impression of the awe reflected in the word-picture of the title, so much do I still admire the wrath of the mighty snow-mountain, that I dare not approach it with the familiarity of a reporter. I see that here and there I have tried to be funny—that is because of the pain in my frozen foot. When I make fun of Mont Blanc I am reminded of an antique bas-relief I once saw in Rome, representing a little grinning Satyr, who, with a grimace of amazement, measures the toe of a sleeping Polyphemus.

THE ascent of Mont Blanc is easy.

No one attempts the Weisshorn, Dent Blanche, or the Matterhorn, unless his eye be steady and his

foot sure, but we all know that Tartarin of Taras-
con went up Mont Blanc—although he never
reached the top.

They are indomitable revolutionists, these other
mountain giants, freedom's untamed heroes who
refuse to be subjugated save by the sun alone,
haughty lords of the Alps who know themselves to
be princes of the blood.

But Mont Blanc is the crowned king of the Alps.
There was a time when he was sullen and cruel, but
he has grown kinder-hearted in his old age, and
now, like a venerable patriarch, he sits there, the
white-haired Charlemagne, looking out in calm
majesty over his three kingdoms.

Good-humouredly he suffers the Lilliputians to
crawl up the marble-bright steps that lead into his
citadel, and with royal hospitality he allows them to
visit his ice-shining castle.

But when the summer day begins to darken into
autumn, he goes to sleep in his white state bed
under a canopy of clouds. And then he does not like
to be disturbed, the old king.

No, he does not like to be disturbed; I knew it
well. I had addressed myself to his retainers and
had been told that it was too late for an audience,
that the king did not receive at this time. I had
come from afar, my knapsack on my back, my head
full of wonderful stories about the far-famed pal-

ace, and longing to see the proud old mountain-king.

Somewhat disconcerted I hung for a while about the castle gates, grumbling socialistic utterances. I had taken in radical newspapers all summer and was not to be treated in that off-hand way. It is the lot of the great to be subjected to the gaze of inquisitive eyes, and I can but be turned away, thought I to myself. And up I went with two followers. Perhaps it was a trifle unceremonious on my part, but I am not used to the court etiquette of conventionality.

Summer, fair daughter of the valley, accompanied me a little way; at first she climbed the slopes easily enough, planting her foot firmly in the clefts, but it was not difficult to see that she did not look forward to the royal visit as ardently as I did. I had got myself up in court dress to pay my respects to the ice-grey monarch, in sharp-spiked mountain shoes, snow gaiters, and steel-pointed pilgrim staff, but she was in no wise equipped to meet the requirements of such a journey, poor little one! The wind pulled and tugged at her leaf-woven petticoat, and sharp stones cut her green velvet shoes adorned with bows of hare-bell and forget-me-not. But she did not give in so easily; she bound her poor feet with soft moss; she patched her petticoat with bracken and juniper, and although her fingers were stiff-frozen, neatly and gracefully she managed to weave some tiny heather-bells between.

And thus we reached the summit of a rock, and on the edge thereof sat Cerberus, the fierce sentinel of the castle, barking and howling and shaking his arctic fur till great white tufts flew in the air around. I have never been afraid of bad-tempered dogs, and hailed old Boreas by his name and asked him in our own language if he did not recognise me, he, the guardian of my childhood's home. And sure enough he rushed at me full speed! He laid his paws upon my breast with such force that he nearly knocked me backward over the cliff, and licked my face with his icy tongue till I could hardly breathe. But suddenly, in the midst of his friendly demonstrations, he bit my nose, and, what is more, he nearly bit it off—that is what I have always said, one cannot be too careful where strange dogs are concerned! If anyone is a lover of dogs I am, but I did not know how to take that, and hurried on as quickly as possible. He evidently thought he belonged to the party, and followed us growling like the brute that he was. But summer grew frightened and said she dared not go any farther, and so we took leave of each other. Light-footed and joyous she returned to the green of the Alpine meadows, and I, drawing my cloak closer round me, went on my way. Some firs also took courage, and, grip-

ping the rugged granite with sinewy arms, they
followed us up the rock.

Steeper and steeper became the track, thinner
and thinner the ranks of the green-clad bodyguard
which advanced with me. And soon the last of them
halted beneath the shelter of a jutting rock. I asked
them if they would not come a little farther, but
they shook their white heads and bade me farewell.
Deeper and deeper penetrated the chill of death
into the mountain's veins; slower and slower beat
the heart of Nature; higher and higher went my
way. And there she stood, the last outpost of Summer, the courageous little child-flower of the mountain heights, beautiful as her name, Edelweiss! She
stood there quite alone with her feet in the snow;
no living soul had she to bear her company, but she
was just as neat for all that in her little grey
woollen gown edged with frost pearls, and just as
frankly for all that did she look up at the sun. She
also had her part to play, and it was not for me to
do her any harm. I glanced at her a moment and
thought how pretty she was, although so simply
clad in her homespun, poor little half-frozen Cin-
derella amongst her summer-fair sisters of the
valley.

I stood now on the frontier of the kingdom of
Eternal Winter, and firm of foot I crossed the
moat of frozen glacier-waves which surrounded the
citadel of the ice-monarch. There reigned a deso-

late repose over the sleeping palace, and I felt that I was drawing nigh unto a king. I wandered through deserted castle-halls on whose dazzling white carpets no human foot had ever trod, beneath crystal-glittering temple vaults through which the organ thundered like the roar of a subterranean river, between tall colonnades whose cloud-hidden capitals supported the firmament.

So I reached the highest tower of the castle. The winding staircase leading thereunto was gone, but with ice-axe and rope we assaulted the Royal Eagle's nest.

And I stood face to face with the mountain-king. Upon the giant's forehead sat the beaming diadem of the sun, and an unspeakable splendour of purple and gold fell over his royal mantle. No echo from the valleys disturbed his proud repose; mournful in isolated peace he sat on high surveying his mute kingdom. Silent stood the bodyguard about his throne, the tall grenadiers with steel-glinting ice armour upon their granite breasts and cloud-crested helmets upon their snow-white heads. I knew the weather-beaten features of more than one of them full well, and reverently I greeted the giants by name, Schreckhorn, Wetterhorn, Finsteraarhorn, Monte Rosa, Monte Viso, and her, the virgin warrior with lowered visor over her beautiful face immaculate as Diana in her snow-white garb, Die Jungfrau! And my eye dwelt long upon the proud combatant yonder, Achilles-like in his god-forged armour purpled with blood, the Matter-horn!

But suddenly the king's face darkened and a sombre cloud fell over his forehead. He took off his crown, and his white curls flew in the wind, and without paying the slightest attention to us he put on his night-cap.[1] And we understood that the audience was ended.

But he must be a good sleeper indeed if he be able to rest in such a noise as this, thought we, for around us there arose a fearful tumult. The storm raged over our heads till we thought the roof of the castle would fall in upon us, and Boreas, like a hungry wolf, howled at our heels. Hastily we retraced our steps through the darkening palace; through deserted courtyards where spirit hands swept every trace of path away; through vast state halls, gloomy as chambers of death in their white draperies; through vaults adown which the organ stormed as on the Day of Judgment.

But there was something wrong with these old castle-halls—I began to think they were haunted. There were groans and shrieks; a shrill and scornful laugh rang suddenly through the air, and beside us flew long shadows swathed in white—it was not

[1] *Il met son bonnet*—the guides' usual and sufficiently characteristic metaphor referring to the little cloud which suddenly covers the summit of Mont Blanc—it announces a storm. It looks its best from a certain distance.

easy to make out what they were; mountain-wraiths, I suppose.

We then reached a big plain called *le grand plateau,* but we had hardly got half-way across it before a cannon shot rent the skies. I looked up to see the white smoke dancing down the Mont Maudit and a whole mountain of projectiles bearing down upon us with the speed of an avalanche— "Sapristi!" On we went. Then there came a crash as though the thunder had burst over our heads, the ground gaped under our feet, and I fell into Hades. Everything became silent and the chill of death fell over me.

But the instinct of self-preservation roused me, and half awake I sat up in the coffin and looked around. At the same moment one of my followers also crept out of his shroud, and by the help of the ice-axe we forced open the lid that had already been screwed down over our third companion. Greatly astonished, we discovered that we were not dead at all. We sat imprisoned in a subterranean dungeon waiting for trial, but we all agreed that we were in the cell of the condemned. Daylight fell through a narrow rift over our heads, and beside us yawned a great chasm—it was like the Mamertine prison in Rome. We had time to meditate upon a good many things. To complain was useless; to protest against our fate was useless too; all we could do was to hope that the judicial formalities might be conducted as quickly as possible.

Now and then a white wraith peeped through the opening and with a mocking laugh threw down great heaps of snow, then swept away over our heads. "Are you still the lords of the earth, you miserable little human microbes?" they roared until the vault shook again. We clenched our teeth and said nothing. At last I got quite angry and shouted back to them that they were nothing but microbes themselves. I glanced at my companions and all three of us made a grimace to show how excellent we thought the joke, but it did not come to much, for the muscles of laughter had been paralysed in our blue faces. But the wraiths seemed taken aback all the same, and, summoning up all my courage, I went on calling out that it was useless to give themselves such airs, that there was something higher than Mont Blanc itself, and I pointed towards a star which just then shone down at us poor devils through the grey fog bars of the opening. I had hardly got the words out of my mouth before the wraiths vanished one and all, and by the light of the brightening evening we saw that they had been transformed into huge blocks of ice, which, impelled by the avalanche, had stopped short at the very edge of the crevasse—witchcraft, nothing but witchcraft! But it was not witchcraft that got us out that time. It was something else that helped us—that which is higher than Mont Blanc.

CHAPTER VII

MENAGERIE

.

VII

MENAGERIE

For a few days only ! ! !

BRUTUS, LION FROM NUBIA.

TIGERS, BEARS, WOLVES.

POLAR BEAR.

MONKEYS, HYÆNAS,
AND OTHER REMARKABLE ANIMALS.

The Lion-Tamer, called

"THE LION KING,"

will enter the Lion's cage at 6 o'clock.

For a few days only ! ! !

THE street boys hold out for a while longer, cold
though the evening be, for the Lion King himself
has already twice appeared on the platform in
riding-boots, and his breast sparkling with decorations, and, besides that, one can distinctly hear the
howling of the animals within the tent.

Yes, it would be a pity to miss an entertainment like this; come let us go in!

It is the Lion King's wife herself who is sitting there selling the tickets, and we gaze at her with a deference due to her rank. She wears gold bracelets round her thick wrists, and a double gold chain glitters beneath her fur cape. But the monkeys who sit there on each side of her chained to their perches with leather straps girt tightly round their stomachs—they wear no fur capes. Their faces are blue with cold, and when they jump up and down to try to keep themselves warm the street boys laugh and the market people stop to have a look at them, poor unconscious clowns of the show who are there for the purpose of luring in spectators to witness the tortures of their other companions in distress.

The tent is full of people, and the many gaslights inflame the polluted air. The show has already begun, and the spectators follow a negro from cage to cage who, pointing a stick at the prisoner behind the bars, in monotonous voice announces his age, his country, and his crime of having led the life which Nature has taught him to live.

I have been here several times, and I know the negro's description by heart. Let me show you the animals.

Here, in this cage, moping on his perch, his head hidden beneath his ragged feather-cloak, you see

the proudest representative of the bird world—
"The Royal Eagle, three years old, taken young."
You have read about him, the strong-winged bird,
who in solemn majesty circles above the desolate
mountain-tops. Alone he lives up there amongst the
clouds—alone like the human soul. He builds his
nest upon an inaccessible rock, and the precipice
shields his young from rapacious hands. "Taken
young"; that means that the nest was plundered,
the mother was shot as she flew shrieking to protect
her young, and by the butt-end of the gun was
broken the wing-bone of the half-grown eagle as he
struggled for his freedom. Here he has sat ever
since; he sleeps during the day, but he is awake the
live-long night, and when all is silent in the tent a
strange uncanny moan may be heard from his cage.
"Three years old!" he is not the most to be pitied
here, for he is not likely to last long—the Royal
Eagle dies when caged.

Here you see a "Bear." His cage is so small that
he cannot walk up and down; he sits there almost
upright on his hind-quarters, rocking his meek and
heavy head from side to side. If you offer him a
piece of bread, he flattens his nose against the bars
and gently and carefully takes the gift out of your
hand. His nose is torn by the iron ring he once
was made to wear, and his eyes are bloodshot and
streaming from the strong gaslight; but their expression is not bad, it is kind and intelligent like

that of an old dog. Now and then he grips the bars
with his mighty paws, helplessly shaking the cage,
until the guinea-pigs who live below him rush up
and down in abject terror. Ay, shake your cage,
old Bruin! the bars are steel, stronger than your
paws; you will never come out—you are to die in
your prison. You are a dangerous beast of prey—
you live on bilberries and fruit, and now and then
you help yourself to a sheep to keep yourself from
dying of starvation. God Almighty did not know
better than to teach you to do so, but no doubt it
was very ill-judged of Him, and you are very much
to blame; it is only man who has the right to eat
his fill.

Here you see a "Hyæna." The negro stirs up the
hyæna with a cut of his whip, and timorously the
animal crouches in the farthermost corner of the
cage, whilst the negro tells the spectators that
the hyæna is known for its cowardice. The hyæna
dare not risk an open fight, but treacherously attacks the defenceless prisoner whom the savages
have left bound hand and foot to his fate in the
wilderness, or the exhausted beast of burden whom
the caravan has abandoned in the desert after having hoisted onto another the load he is no longer
able to bear. The negro pokes cautiously with his
pointed stick into the corner where the cowardly
animal tries to hide itself, and the spectators all
agree that the hyæna, with its crouching back and

restless eyes, conveys a faithful picture of treachery
and cowardice. Few of the spectators have ever
seen a hyæna before, but they have seen crouching
backs and restless eyes. Not even the dead does the
hyæna leave in peace, says the negro, and with dis-
gust man turns away from the guilty animal.

Here you see a "Polar Bear." Its name is advertised in huge letters on the placard outside; and he
deserves the distinction well indeed, for his torture
perhaps surpasses that of all the other animals.
The Polar bear is another dangerous beast of prey;
he does a little fishing for himself up in the north,
where man is busy exterminating the whales with
dynamite. The horrible sufferings of the animal
need no comment—let us go on.

A little "South African Monkey" and a rabbit
live next to the cage inhabited by the panting Polar
bear.[1]

The little monkey is sick to death of the eternal
clambering up and down the bars of the cage, and
the swing which dangles over her head does not
amuse her any more. Sadly she sits there upon her
straw-covered prison floor, in one hand she holds a
half-withered carrot, which she turns over once
again to see if it looks equally unappetising on
every side, while with the other she sorrowfully
scratches the rabbit's back. Now and then she gets

[1] Perhaps you are not aware of the common practice in menageries
of keeping a rabbit in the monkey's cage for the sake of warmth.

interested, drops the carrot, and attentively with both hands explores some suspicious-looking spot on her companion's mangy back and pulls out a few hairs, which she attentively examines. But soon she wearies of the rabbit also, and does not know in the least what to do with herself. She looks round in the straw, but there is nothing to be seen but the carrot; she looks round the bare, slippery walls of her cage, but neither there is there anything of the slightest interest to be found. And at last she has nothing else to do but, for the hundredth time that hour, to jump into the swing, only to leap on to the floor the next minute and seat herself again, leaning against the rabbit. The spectators call this jumping for joy, but the poor little monkey knows how jolly it is. The rabbit is resigned. The captivity of generations has stupefied him—the longing for liberty has died ages ago from out of his degenerated hare-brain. He hopes for nothing, but he desires nothing. He has no social talents; he is in no way qualified to entertain his restless friend; and besides that, he entirely fails to grasp the situation. But he rewards the monkey to the best of his abilities for the little offices of friendship which she performs for him; and when the gas has been turned out, and the cold night air enters the tent, then the Northerner lends his warm fur coat to the trembling little Southerner, and nestling close to one another they await the new day.

The inhabitant of the cage in yonder corner has not been advertised at all upon the placard outside. He is not to be seen just now; perhaps he is asleep for a while in his dark, little bedroom; but every one who catches sight of that wire wheel knows that it is a "Squirrel" who lives here. What he has to do in a menagerie is more than I can say, for on that point the Zoological education of the public should surely be completed—we all know what the squirrel looks like. Superstitious people of my country say that it is an evil omen if a squirrel crosses their path. I don't know where they got hold of that idea, but maybe they have taken it from a squirrel—for the squirrel believes exactly the same thing if a man crosses his path, and, alas! he has got reason enough for his belief. I, on the contrary, have always thought it a piece of good luck whenever I have happened to come across a little squirrel. Often enough while roaming through the woods and halting with grateful joy at every other step before some new wonder in the fairyland of nature—often enough have I caught a glimpse of the graceful, nimble little fellow swinging himself high overhead on some leafy branch, or carefully peeping out from his little twig cottage, watching with his bright eyes whether any schoolboys were lurking beneath his tree. "Come along, little man," I then would say in squirrel language; "true enough, I did not turn out the man I had been expected to become when

at school; but, thank God! I have at least arrived
so far in knowledge that I have learned to feel
tender sympathy for you and yours!" We were,
alas! not taught this at school in my days; we exchanged birds' eggs for old stamps; we shot small
birds with guns as big as ourselves—and now let
him who can, come and deny the doctrine of original
sin! We were cruel to animals, like all savages. To
the best of my abilities do I now endeavour to ex-
piate the wrong I was then guilty of. But an evil
action never dies; and I know of bloodstains on
tiny boys' fingers which have rusted to stains of
shame in the childhood recollections of the man.
To my humiliation I have shot many a little bird,
and many another did I keep imprisoned. Regret-
fully do I also own to having killed a squirrel;
treacherously did I plunder his home, and his little
one did I imprison in just such another cage as the
one we now stand in front of. See! there comes the
little squirrel out from his bedroom and begins to
run round and round in his wire wheel. He has
made the same attempt thousands and thousands of
times, and yet he makes it once again. Yes, it looks
very pretty! when I used to watch my squirrel running round and round in his wire wheels in precisely
the same way, and at last the wheel was turning so
rapidly that I could not distinguish the bars, I
thought it was capital fun. I know now why he
runs; he runs in anxious longing for freedom; he

runs as long as he has strength to run; for neither
is he able to distinguish any more the bars of the
turning wheel. He may run a mile and still he is
hedged in by the same prison bars. The simple invention is almost diabolically cunning; it is the
wheel of Ixion in the Tartarus of pain to which
mankind has banished animals.

Here you see a "Wolf from Siberia." The wolf
is also, as is well known, a dangerous, wild beast.
When the cold is extreme, and the snow lies very
deep, the wolves approach the habitation of man,
and in starving crowds they follow any sledge they
meet—they have even been known in very rare
cases to attack the horses. We have all read that
terrible story of the Russian peasant on his way
home across the deserted snow-fields; he heard the
panting of the wolves behind his sledge, and he
could see their eyes glitter through the darkness of
the night, so in order to save his own life he had to
throw one of his children to the wolves.

The negro informs you that the wild beast in this
cage was caught young; the she-wolf as usual was
killed while attempting to save her cub.

The bottom of the cage is shining like a parquet
floor from the continual tramping up and down of
the prisoner within, for he knows no rest. Night and
day he paces to and fro, his head bent low as
though in search of some outlet of escape; he will
never find it; he will die behind those bars even as

the prisoners in his own country die in their irons.

The big "Parrot" on her perch over there sheds the one ray of light on this dark picture. The parrot I need not describe to you, for you know the species well. This one hails, we are told, from the New World, but one comes across a good many parrots in the Old World also. The parrot is a universal favourite, and is to be found in nearly every house. The parrot is not unhappy; she is unconscious of the chain round her leg; she does not realise that she was born with wings. She is undisturbed by any unnecessary brain activity; she eats, she sleeps, trims her gorgeous feather cloak, and chatters ceaselessly from morning till night. Left to herself she is silent, for she is only able to repeat what others have said before her, and this she does so cleverly, that often, on hearing some one chatter, I have to ask myself whether it be a human being or a parrot. . . .

The ragged, attenuated animal standing over there and gazing at us with her soft, sad eyes is a "Chamois from Switzerland." The chamois is a rarity in a menagerie, for, as is well known, it usually frets to death during the first year of its captivity. I look at the poor animal with a feeling of oppression at my heart which you can scarcely realise. I have breathed the free air of the high mountains myself, and I know why the chamois dies in prison. Those were other times, poor captive chamois, when you were roving on the Alpine meadows amidst rhododendrons and myrtillus; when on high, over a precipice, I saw your beautiful silhouette standing out against the clear, bright sky! You had no need of an alpen-stock, you, to climb up there, where I watched the aerial play of your graceful limbs amongst the rocks. Up to the realm of ice you led the way, high on the slopes of Monte Rosa has my clumsy, human foot trodden the snow in the track of your dainty mountain shoes. Ay, those were other times, poor prisoner! Those were other times both for you and me, and we had better say no more about them.

Yonder stalwart, muscular ape is a "Baboon"; "Aged Abyssinian Male" stands written under his cage. He sits there, wrapped in thought, fingering a straw. Now and then he casts a rapid glance around him, and be sure he is not so absent-minded as he looks. The eye is intelligent, but malevolent; its owner is a candidate for humanity.

When the negro approaches his cage he shows him a row of teeth not very unlike the negro's own —the family likeness between the two faces is, for the matter of that, unmistakable. The negro cautions the public against accepting the wrinkled hand which the old baboon extends between the bars. I always treat him to an extra lump of sugar ever since the negro told me he once bit off the thumb of an old woman who poked her umbrella

at him. Besides, I look at him with veneration, for
he comes from an illustrious family. Who knows
whether he is not an ill-starred descendant of that
heroic old baboon whom Brehm once met in Abyssinia? The negro is sure to know nothing of that
story, so I may as well tell it you. One day, while
travelling in Abyssinia, the great German nat-
uralist fell in with a whole troop of baboons, who,
bound for some high rocks, were marching along
a narrow defile. The rear had not yet emerged from
the defile when the dogs of Brehm and his companions rushed forward and barred their passage.
Seeing the danger, the other baboons, who had
already reached the rocks, then descended in a body
to the rescue of the attacked, and they screamed so
terribly that the dogs actually fell back. The whole
troop of baboons was now filing off in perfect order
when the dogs were again set at them. All the apes,
however, reached the rocks in safety, with the exception of one half-year-old baboon who happened
to have been lagging behind; he was surrounded
on all sides by the open-mouthed dogs, and with
loud cries of distress he jumped on to a big boulder.
At this juncture a huge baboon stepped down from
the rocks for the second time, advanced alone to
the stone where the little one was crouching, patted
him on the back, lifted him gently down, and so
led him off triumphantly before the very noses of
the dogs, who were so taken by surprise that it never

even occurred to them to attack him. One need not have read Darwin to pronounce that baboon a hero.

I have noticed that even kind-hearted spectators do not seem to feel very much commiseration for captive monkeys. The ape plays in the menagerie the same rôle as Don Quixote in literature—the superficial observer looks upon them as exclusively comical, and only laughs at them. But the attentive looker-on knows that the solitary monkey's life behind the bars is in its way nothing but a tragedy, as well as Cervantes' immortal book is nothing but a mournful epic. With tender emotion he feels how an increasing sympathy mingles in his pitiful smile the more he gets to know of them— these two superannuated types: Don Quixote, the simple-minded would-be hero, still lagging on the scene long after the epopee of chivalry has departed in the twilight of mediæval mysticism; and the ape, the phantom from the vanishing animal world, over whose hairy human face already falls the dawn of the birth day of the First Man.

This baboon may perhaps appear to you very ugly; but we know that the appreciation of physical beauty is an entirely individual one, and it is quite possible that the baboon on his side finds us very ugly. You cannot help smiling now and then when standing and watching him, but, at least, try not to let him see it, for, like all monkeys, it irritates him to be laughed at to his face. This old baboon

is deeply unhappy, for, as he has got more brains
than the other animals in the menagerie, his capacity
for suffering is consequently greater—for we all
know that suffering is an intellectual function. He
alone realises the hopelessness of his situation, and
his restless brain-activity refuses him the relative
oblivion which resignation vouchsafes to many
others of his companions in distress.

But as a compensation he possesses one quality
which the other animals lack, and it is the posses-
sion of this quality which saves him from falling
into hypochondria. It is his sense of humour.
That the monkey is a born humourist every one
knows who has had the opportunity of observing
him in society—for instance, in the monkey-house
at the Zoo. This sense of humour does not even
desert the poor monkey kept in solitary confine-
ment. And sometimes when I have been standing
here for a while watching the mimicry of this old
baboon, I have involuntarily had to ask myself
whether he were not making fun of me. . . .

The negro has finished his recital, and it is time
for the show-piece of the evening to come off.
The spectators crowd in front of the lion-cage,
dividing their admiration between Brutus, the
Nubian lion behind the bars, and the keeper, who,
unarmed, is about to enter the cage. The man
throws off his overcoat, and the "Lion King"
stands before us in all his pride—pink tights, rid-

ing-boots, and his gold-laced breast covered with decorations—from Nubia likewise even these. He is small of stature, like Napoleon, and the constant intercourse with the wild beasts has given his face a rough and repulsive expression. He reeks of brandy, to counteract the stale smell of the cage, and his pomatumed hair curls neatly round his low-sloping forehead. The negro hands him a whip, and the solemn moment is at hand. Proudly the Lion King creeps into the cage, and proudly he cracks his whip at the half-sleeping Brutus. The lion raises himself with a sullen roar, and, hugging the walls, begins to wander round his cage. Proudly the Lion King stretches out his whip, and obediently, like a dog, Brutus leaps lazily over it. Proudly the negro hands his master a hoop, and wearily and dejectedly Brutus jumps through it. Brutus is sulky to-night; he does not roar as he ought to do. Things look up, however, towards the end of the performance, when the Lion King, standing in a corner of the cage, paralyses Brutus with a proud look just as he is about to attack him. Brutus is no longer obstinate, but roars irreproachably, and shows his yellow fang. A few half-smothered cries of alarm are heard from the audience, an old woman faints, a pistol is fired off, while the Lion King, under cover of the smoke, hurriedly and proudly creeps out of the cage.

Captive lion, have you then forgotten that once you were a King yourself, that once there was a time when all men trembled at your approach, that the forest grew silent when your imperious voice resounded? Fallen monarch, awake from the degradation of your thraldom; rise to combat, and let the thunder of your royal voice be heard once more!

Brutus, Brutus, vindicator of lost freedom, you are too proud to be a slave! Rend asunder the chains which coward human cunning has bound around the sleeping power of your limbs!

Shake that flaming lion mane of yours, and, strong as Samson in your mighty wrath, bring down the prison walls around you to crush the Philistines assembled here to jeer at the impotence of their once-dreaded enemy!

Brutus, Brutus, vindicator of lost freedom!

CHAPTER VIII

ZOOLOGY

VIII

ZOOLOGY

THEY say that love for mankind is the highest of
all virtues. I admire this love for mankind, and I
know well that it is an attribute of noble minds.
My soul is too small, my thoughts fly too near the
earth ever to reach so far, and I am obliged to
acknowledge that the longer I live the farther I
depart from this high ideal. I should lie if I said
that I love mankind.

But I love animals, oppressed, despised animals,
and I do not care when people laugh at me because
I say that I get on better with them than with the
majority of people I come across.

When one has been talking to somebody for
half an hour, one has, as a rule, had quite enough—
isn't it so? I, at least, usually feel inclined to slip
away then, and I am always astonished that the
person I have been speaking with has not tried to
escape long before. But I am never bored in the
society of a friendly dog, even if I do not know
him or he me. Often, when I meet a dog walking
along by himself, I stop and ask him where he is
going, and have a little chat with him; and even if

no further conversation takes place, it does me good to look at him, and try to enter into the thoughts which are working in his mind. Dogs have this immense advantage over man, that they cannot dissimulate; and Talleyrand's paradox, that language was invented in order to conceal our thoughts, cannot be applied to dogs.

I can sit half the day in a field watching the grazing cattle; and to observe the physiognomy of a little donkey is one of the keenest pleasures of a psychologist. But it is specially when donkeys are free that they are most interesting: a tied-up donkey is not nearly so communicative and natural as when she is left to herself; and that, after all, is not much to be wondered at.

At Ischia I once lived for a long time almost exclusively with a donkey. It was Fate which brought us together. I had put up at a little boat-house down at the Marina, and the donkey lived next door to me. I had quite lost my sleep up in the stifling rooms of the hotel, and had gladly accepted my friend Antonio's invitation to live down at the Marina in his cool boat-house, while he was out fishing in the bay of Gaeta. I fared exceedingly well in there amongst the pots and fishing-nets; and astride the keel of an old upturned boat I wrote long love-letters to the sea. And when evening came and it began to grow dusk in the boat-house, I went to bed in my hammock, with a

sail for a covering and the memory of a happy day
for a pillow. I fell asleep with the waves, and I
awoke with the day. Each morning came my neighbour, the old donkey, and stuck in her solemn head
through the open door, looking steadfastly at me.
I always wondered why she stood there so still and
did nothing but stare at me, and I could not hit
upon any other explanation than that she thought
I was nice to look at. I lay there half-awake watching her—I thought that she too was nice to look at.
She looked like an old family portrait as she stood
there with her grey head framed by the doorway
against the blue background of a summer's morning. Out there it grew lighter and lighter, and the
clear surface of the sea began to glitter. Then came
a ray of sunlight dancing right into my eyes, and
I sprang up and greeted the gulf. I had nothing
whatever to do all day, but the poor donkey should,
as a matter of fact, have been at work the whole
forenoon up in Casamicciola. However, such a
sympathy sprang up between us, that I got her
a *locum tenens,* and then we wandered light-
heartedly about all day long, like true vagabonds,
wherever the road led us. Sometimes it was I who
walked ahead, with the donkey trotting quietly at
my heels; sometimes it was she who had got a fixed
determination of her own, and then I naturally
followed her. The whole time I studied with great
attention the interesting personality I had so un-

expectedly come across, and it was long since I had found myself in such congenial company. I might have much more to say about all this, but these psychological researches may prove far too serious a topic for many of my readers, and I therefore believe I had better stop here.

And the birds—who can ever tire of them? Hour after hour I can sit on a mossy stone and listen to what a dear little bird has to say—I, who can never keep my thoughts together when some one is talking to me. But have you noticed how sweet a little bird is to look at when he sings his song, and now and again bends his graceful head, as if to listen for some one to answer far away in the forest? In the late summer, when the bird-mother has to teach her children to talk—do not believe it is only a matter of instinct, even they have to take lessons in learning their singing language—have you watched these lessons, when the mother from her swinging chair lectures about something or other, and the summer-old little ones stammer after her with their clear child-voices?

And when the birds are silent, I have only to look down in the grass and moss to light on other acquaintances to keep me company. Over waving grass and corn flies a dragon-fly on wings of sun-glitter and fairy-web, and deep down on the path, which winds between the huge stems of grass, a little ant toils along with a dry fir-needle on her back. Rough is the road: now it goes up-hill and now it goes down-hill, now she pushes the heavy load like a sledge before her, now she carries it upon her slender shoulders. She pulls so hard up-hill that her little legs stiffen, she rolls down the steep slopes with her burden clasped tightly in her arms; but she never lets go, and on she struggles, for she is in a hurry to get home. Soon the dew will fall, and then it is unsafe to be out in the trackless forest, and best to be home in peace after the day's work is ended. Now the road becomes hilly, and suddenly a mighty mountain stops the way—what the mountain is called the ant knows well enough; I know nothing, and to me it looks like a pebble no bigger than my fist. The ant stops short and ponders awhile, then she gives a signal with her antennæ, which I am too dull to understand, but which others at once respond to, for from behind a dry leaf I see two other ants advance to the rescue. I watch how they hold a council of war, and how the new arrivals with great concern pull the log to try how heavy it is. Suddenly they stand quite still and listen—an ant-patrol is marching along a little way off, and I see how another couple of ants are told off to lend assistance. Then they all take hold together, and, like sailors, they haul up the log with a long, slow pull.

I understand it is to repair the havoc made by an earthquake that the log is to be used. How many hard-working lives were perhaps crushed under the ruins of the fallen houses? and what evil power was it that destroyed what so much patient labour built up? I dare not ask, for who knows if it were not a passing man who amused himself by knocking down the ant-hill with his stick!

And all the other tiny creatures, whose names I do not know, but into whose small world I look with joy, they also are fellow-citizens in Creation's great society, and probably they fulfil their public duties far better than I fulfil mine!

And besides, when thus lying down and staring into the grass, one ends by becoming so very small oneself.

And at last it seems to me as if I myself were nothing but an ant, struggling on with my heavy load through the trackless forest. Now it goes up-hill, and now it goes down-hill. But the thing is not to let go. And if there is some one to help to give a pull where the hill seems too steep and the load too heavy, all goes well enough.

But suddenly Fate passes by and knocks down all that has been built up with so much hard labour.

The ant struggles on with her heavy load deep in the trackless forest. The way is long, and there is still some time before the day's work is over and the dew falls.

But high overhead flies the dream on wings of sun-glitter and fairy-web.

CHAPTER IX

A CRY IN THE WILDERNESS.

IX

A CRY IN THE WILDERNESS

WE LEARN from the long history of the development of our race that the hunter stage was the lowest of all human conditions—the almost purely animal. The wild beast's lust for blood has gradually evolved into an unconscious instinct, and thousands of years of culture lie between our savage ancestors who slew each other with stone axes for a piece of raw fish, and the animal-hunter of to-day. The method has been refined, but the principle remains the same—the same impulse of the stronger to slay the weaker, which runs through the whole animal series. The passion for killing being an animal instinct, is, as such, impossible to eradicate. But it behoves man, conscious of his high rank, to struggle against this vice of his wild childhood, the phantom from the grave where sleep the progenitors of his race. Man's right to kill animals is limited to his right of defence and his right of existence. The former can only be evoked in exceptional cases in our countries, the latter cannot be evoked by our class.

The man of culture admits his obligations towards animals in compensation for the servitude he imposes on them. The killing of animals for mere pleasure is incompatible with the fulfilment of these obligations. Sympathy extending beyond the range of humanity, *i.e.,* kindness to animals, is one of the last moral qualities acquired by mankind; and the more this sympathy is developed in man, the greater is the distance which separates him from his primitive state of savagery. The individual in which this sympathy is lacking is thus to be considered as a transitional type between the savage and the civilised man. He forms the missing link in the evolution of the human mind from brutishness to culture.

·   ·   ·   ·   ·   ·

It was never meant that man should be an autocratic tyrant in the great society which peoples the world, but a constitutional monarch. I had dreamt of a republic, but I admit that our planet is not yet ripe for this form of government. Yes, man is the ruler of the earth. Always victorious, he carries his blood-stained banner round the world, and there is no longer any limit to his kingdom. But man is an upstart—I, for one, am not taken in by all his boasting over his high birth. He tries to make us believe that he is a foundling who was mysteriously deposited in the nursery of creation, and that he is

of far nobler origin than anybody else on the whole
earth. It is true there is something peculiar about
him; and that he is domineering and arrogant he
showed early enough. Already, as a mere man-cub
at the mother-breast of Nature, he pushed aside the
other children of the earth, and drank the strength
of life in deep draughts. Hardly could he crawl
before he scratched his kind nurse in the face and
bit his weaker foster-brothers. So he grew up to be
a true bully, a brutish Protanthropos, breaking
down each obstacle, subduing with the right of the
stronger all opposition. And the law of selection
enlarged his facial angle, and culture put arms in
his hands. How could the sickle-like claws of *Ursus
spelaeus* (cave-bear) prevail against his trident
studded with thorns or twig-spikes or set with
razor-edged shells? What could the six-inch-long
canines of Machærodus do against his sharpened
flint? And so they disappeared, one after the other,
these vanquished giants, into the gloom of past
ages. But the power of man expanded more and
more, and higher and higher flew his thoughts. The
earth lies at his feet, and he now prepares to assault
heaven! And he has been so spoilt by all his success,
so refined by all civilisation, that he turns up his
aristocratic nose whenever one reminds him of his
humble old ancestors, among whom his cradle stood,
and of his poor relations who, homeless, rove about
the earth, and to whom he is so hard. But man is

no longer young—no one knows exactly how many
hundred thousand years he carries on his shoulders;
and I think it is time for him to reflect a little upon
all the evil he has done in his days, and to try to
be somewhat kinder in his old age. The day will
come when the last man will lie down to die, and
when a new-crowned king of creation will mount
the throne—*le roi est mort, vive le roi!*

The twilight of ages falls round the sarcophagus
where the dead monarch sleeps in the Pantheon of
Palæontology. Dust covers the inscription which
records the honorary titles of the dead, and the
banners which witnessed his victories moulder
away. Up there in the new planet sits a professor,
and lectures on the remains from prehistoric times,
and he hands round to his audience a fragile
cranium, which is carefully examined by wondering
students. It is our cranium, with that upright
facial angle and that large brain-pan which was
our pride! And the professor makes a casual remark about *Homo Sapiens,* and he points out the
fang which is still to be seen in the jaw.

CHAPTER X

POLITICAL AGITATIONS IN CAPRI

Political Agitations in Capri

Don't be alarmed—they are not going to disturb the peace of Europe.

Alas! there are spots even on the sun, and neither is "the loveliest pearl in Naples' crown" altogether faultless.

Croaking ravens swarm around the ruins where thousand-year-old memories lie slumbering, dirty dwarf hands fumble amidst the remains of fallen giants' vanished splendour, barbarians pull to pieces the mosaic floors on which the feet of emperors trod. Night-capped and blue-stockinged Prose startles the Idyll which lies there dreaming with half-closed eyes, grinning fauns bend asunder the vines which hide from view the cool grotto where the nymph of the legend bathes her graceful limbs.

Capri is sick, Capri is infested with parasites even as the old lion. Capri is full of—yes, but in politics one has to be careful. I say nothing; read the article to the end, and you will see what it is that Capri is full of.

Amidst the ruins of Tiberius's Villa you sit on

high, gazing out over the sea. Absently your eye follows a white sail in the distance; it is a little peaceful fishing-boat quietly sailing home. And your thoughts wander far, far away. Here, in his marble-shining palace, stood once upon a time the ruler of the world; he gazed out over the sea, as you do, but his eye was not as fearless as yours, for he dreaded the avenger of his victims in every approaching boat; and when the bay was dark he would still linger up there and, trembling, seek to read his doom in the stars which studded the vault of heaven. No crimes could help him any longer to forgetfulness of himself; no vice could any more benumb the torture of his soul. Within his rock-built citadel the sombre emperor suffered torments far greater than any he had ever inflicted on his victims; his heart had long since bled to death under his purple toga, but his soul lived on in its titanic sorrow. The spot whereon you lie is named "Il Salto di Tiberio." From here he hurled his victims into the sea, and there below men were rowing about in boats in order to crush to death with their oars those who were still struggling with the waves. Bend over the precipice and see the foaming surge—old fishermen have told me that sometimes when the moon goes under a cloud and all is dark, the waves breaking over the rocks beneath seem tinged with blood.

But the sun streams his forgiveness over the crumbled witness of so much sin, and, ere long, the vision of the sombre emperor fades from your thought. Now it is silent and peaceful up at Villa Tiberio. You lie there on your back gazing out over the gulf, and it seems to you as though the world ended beyond its lovely shores. The restless strife of the day does not reach you here, and all dissonance is silenced; your thoughts fly aimlessly round, play for awhile amongst the surf near Sorrento's rocks, send their open-armed greeting to Ischia's groves, and pluck some fragrant roses from the verdant shore of Posilipo. So perception gradually dies away, no longer do you hear the buzz of the whirling wheels in the factory of thought—to-day is a day of rest, and your soul may dream. What dream you? You know not! Where are you? You know not! You fly on the white wings of the sea-gulls, far, far away over the wide waters; you sail with the brilliant clouds high overhead, where no thought can reach you.

But you are only a prisoner after all—a prisoner who dreamt he was free and is awakened in the midst of his dreams by the rattle of a jailer's key. The sound of voices strikes your ear, and like a wing-shot bird you fall to the earth. Beside you stands a lanky individual, and he says to his companion that it is incredible that a man can be prosaic

enough to fall asleep on a spot so "wunderbar."
Ah, you are asleep, are you?

The spell is broken, the harmony destroyed, and
you get up to go away. He then assaults you with
the question whether you don't think the gulf is
blue? and you have not walked on ten yards before
he attacks you treacherously from behind with the
remark that the sky is also blue. You believe it
helps to stare savagely at him—I have done it many
times, and it does not impress him in the very least.
You want to try to make him believe you are deaf
—that is no use either; he takes it as a compliment,
for he prefers to have the conversation all to
himself.

The sun stands high in the heavens and the
summer's day is so warm—come, let us go and
bathe in the cool water of the Blue Grotto. No, my
friend, not there! Even thither, like sharks, they
come swimming after us to ask us if we are aware
that the Blue Grotto of Capri is virtually German,
that it was "ein Deutscher" who discovered the
grotto in 1826. Let us be off for "Bagni di Tiberio"
—the ruins of the emperor's bath—strip off our
clothes inside one of the cool little chambers which
still remain amongst huge blocks of crumbling
masonry, and plunge into the sapphire water. But
do you see those huge holes in the fine sand? Alas,
my friend, let us be off! I know the track, and there

she sits, the blonde Gretchen, reading one of Spiel-
hagen's novels—were it Heine she was reading I
might perhaps forgive her.

We return along the beach to the Marina, and
wend our way along the old path between the vineyards leading up to the village. Unfortunately the
new carriage road is nearly ready, but we, of course,
prefer the old way, by far the more picturesque
of the two. On the beach we stumble over easels
and colour-boxes at short distances, set out as traps
for dreamers; beside each trap sits an amateur in
ambush under a big umbrella, and he invokes "Der
Teufel" to help him, which I suppose he does.

You propose putting up at Albergo Pagano—
yes, you are quite right; it is no doubt the best
hotel in the island. Old Pagano, who was a capital
fellow, died many years ago, and only we old
Capriotes can remember him. His son Manfredo,
who now manages the hotel, is my very good friend;
but it is not his fault that his house has become as
German as though it lay in the heart of "Das grosse
Vaterland." At least a good fifty of them are gathered round the table in the big dining-room. Upon
the walls hangs a plaster medallion of the "Kaiser,"
decorated with fresh laurels; and should they pay
you the compliment of mistaking you for a French-
man, it is just possible they may drink a bumper
to the memory of 1870—an experience I once went
through myself. Instead of the silence and peace

you so longed for, you are subjected during the
whole of dinner-time to the most terrific uproar,
worthy of a "Kneipe" in Bremen. In despair you
fling open the door leading into the garden—no,
you are in Italy after all! Out there under the pergola the moonbeams are playing amongst the vines,
the air is soft and caressing, and the summer evening recites to you its enchanting sonnet as a compensation for the prose within. You wander there
up and down all alone, but scarcely have you had
time to say to yourself that you are happy, before

"Heil dir im Sieges Kranz!"

rings like a war-cry through the peaceful night,
echoed from the street by some little Capriote
ragamuffins with a horrible chorus of

"Ach! du lieber Augustin!
Augustin, Augustin!"

.   .   .   .   .   .

Of course I am aware of the supercilious way in
which many of the readers of *Letters from a
Mourning City* [1] have turned up their noses at my
circle of friends out here—lazzaroni, shabby old
monks, half-starving sailors, etc. The hour is at
hand for introducing you to some acquaintances of
mine of somewhat higher rank, and now I will tell
you a story of the upper regions of society. It

[1] *Letters from a Mourning City,* by Axel Munthe. John Murray:
London, 1899.

happened at Capri a good many years ago, and the *dramatis personæ* consisted of my friend D——, myself, and the late Empress Frederic, then Crown Princess of Germany.

My friend D—— and I happened to be the only profane people in the hotel just then. The whole of the big dining-table was in the hands of the Germans, whilst we two sat by ourselves at a small side-table. It was there we had our little observatory, as Professor Palmieri had his on Mount Vesuvius. For some days past our keen instruments of perception had warned us that something unusual was going on at the big table. The roaring of an evening was louder than ever, the smoke rose in thicker clouds, the beer ran in streams, and the faces were flushed to red-heat—everything announced an eruption of patriotism. One evening there arrived a telegram which, amidst a terrific babel of voices, was read aloud by one of the party —a commercial traveller from Potsdam, whom I personally hated, because he snored at night: his room was next to mine, and the walls of the hotel are thin. The telegram announced that the Crown Princess of Germany who had been spending the last few days in Naples, was expected to visit Capri the next day in the strictest incognito. Nobody appeared to understand that the word "incognito" means that one wishes to be left in peace, and during the rest of the dinner the faithful patriots did nothing but discuss the best way of how to spoil the unfortunate Princess's little visit to the island. A complete programme was drawn up there and then: a triumphal arch was to be erected, a select deputation was to swoop down upon her the moment she set foot on land, while the main body was to block her way up to the piazza. Patriotic songs were to be sung in chorus, a speech read, whilst the commercial traveller from Potsdam was to confirm in a welcoming poem what his face already expressed eloquently enough—that poetry was not in his line. Every garden in Capri was to be despoiled of its roses, whole bushes and trees were to be uprooted wherewith to deck the triumphal arch, and all night they were to weave garlands and stitch flags.

I went up to my room, threw myself on the sofa, and lit a cigarette. And as I lay there meditating, feelings of the deepest compassion towards the Crown Princess of Germany began to overwhelm me. I had just read in the papers how, during her stay in Naples, she had sought by every manner of means to elude all official recognition, and to avoid every sort of demonstration in her honour during her excursions round the bay. Poor Princess! she had flattered herself upon having left all weary court etiquette behind in foggy Berlin, and yet she was not to be allowed to enjoy in peace one single summer day on the gulf! To be rich enough to be

able to buy the whole of Capri, and yet be unable
to live the peaceful idyll of the enchanting island
for one short hour! To be destined to wear one
of the proudest crowns of the world, and yet be
powerless to prevent a commercial traveller from
writing poetry! My compassionate reflections were
here disturbed by the noise of heavy footsteps in
the adjoining room; it sounded like the tramp of
horses' hoofs; it was the "Probenreiter" who
mounted his Pegasus. The whole night through I
lay there reflecting on the vanity of earthly power,
and the whole night did the poet-laureate wander
up and down his room. Once the tramping ceased,
and there was a silence. There was a panting from
within, and I heard a husky voice murmur—

> "Ich stehe hier auf Felsenstrand!
> Ich stehe hier auf Felsenstrand!" [1]

A moment afterwards I heard him fling open his
window and let the night air cool the fire of his
inspiration. Our rooms opened on to the same
balcony, and carefully lifting up my blind, I could
see the moonlight falling full upon him as he
leaned against the window frame. His hair stood
on end, and an inarticulate mumble fell from his
lips. He gazed in despair up to the heavens, where
the stars were twinkling knowingly at one another; he glanced out over the garden, where the

[1] "Here I stand on a rocky shore!"

night wind flew tittering amongst the leaves. But
he never saw the joke until a startled young cock
inquired of some old cocks down in the poultry
yard what time it was, and then crowed straight
into his face that the night was passed, and he had
got no further than the first verse. Then he groaned
once more a plaintive

"Ich stehe hier auf Felsenstrand!"

and banged his windows to. All the cocks of
Pagano's crowed "Bravo! bravo!" but Phœbus,
Phœbus Apollo, the god of the Sun and of the
poets, entered his room at that moment, and he red-
dened with anger when he caught sight of the commercial traveller tampering with his lyre.

Later on, when the chambermaid appeared, I
heard him call out for coffee and cognac. Having
spent the whole night like that on his "Felsenstrand," no wonder he needed a pick-me-up.

He was late for luncheon. I glanced at the poet;
an interesting pallor lent a faint look of distinction
to the commercial traveller's plump features, and
his great goggle eyes lay like extinct suns under his
heavy eyelids. He was the object of great attention
from everybody, especially from the fair sex. I
heard him confide to his neighbour at table that he
always succeeded best with improvisations, and that
he did not intend to let the reins of his inspiration
loose until the last moment. They drank to his

charming talent, whereupon he modestly smiled. He ate nothing, but drank considerably. At dessert he had regained his high colour, harangued every one excitedly, and drank toasts right and left. But it seemed as if he dared not be alone with his thoughts; as soon as the conversation around him ceased, he sank into profound meditation, and an attentive observer could easily detect that the roses of his cheeks were hiding cruel thorns which pierced his soul. For it was twelve o'clock; the Princess was expected at four, and he still stood there like Napoleon on St. Helena, alone and abandoned on his "Felsenstrand," vainly gazing out over the unfathomable ocean of poetry in search of one single little friendly rhyme to row him over to the next verse.

The hotel had become quite unbearable downstairs; rehearsals of patriotic songs were going on in the drawing-room, whilst the hall was turned into a busy manufactory of flags and garlands, to which the victim's name and long fluttering ribbons were being attached. The piazza was gaily decorated; the triumphal arch was ready—a black cardboard eagle perched on the top holding in his beak a white placard, upon which stood out in huge red letters the word "Willkommen." Flag-staffs and garlands all over the piazza; even Nicolino, barber and "salassatore" (bleeder), had decided to join the triple alliance, and a colossal German flag was waving before his *salone*. I did not know what to do with myself, and at last I strolled up towards Villa di Tiberio—up there there might be a little chance of peace at all events. I had scarcely had time to lie down in my favourite place far out on the edge of the cliff, viewing the Bay of Naples on one side and the Bay of Salerno and the wide sea on the other, before a long shadow fell across me. I looked up and saw a patriot staring fixedly through a telescope towards Naples. As a matter of fact, something was visible in the midst of the bay, but the haze made it difficult to see what it was. Suddenly he gave a sort of war-whoop, whereupon two other spies, who must have been sitting at the top of the old watch-tower, came bursting on the scene. I knew quite well what it was that had appeared in sight—it was the big "Scoppa" boat sailing home from Naples.[1] Of course I took good care to say nothing, as there was always the faint hope that they might mistake it for the expected steamer, and dash off to the Marina. But unfortunately they also guessed rightly, and all three sat down on the grass beside me, and began munching sandwiches and abusing Tiberius. I took myself off, and returned to Capri. On the piazza I came across my friend D——, who did not seem to be in a very good temper either; he was on his

---

[1] The old means of communication between Capri and Naples. Unfortunately replaced by an ugly little steamer.

way to the Marina, and I accompanied him thither.
Down at the Marina everything was peaceful and
quiet, for the time being at all events. Old men sat
there in the open boat-houses mending their nets,
and small boys, who had not seen fit to put on more
clothes than usual for the Princess's expected visit,
played about in the surf, and rolled their little
bronze bodies in the sand. The landing place was
crowded as is usual when the Naples steamer is
expected; girls stood there offering corals, flowers,
and fruit for sale, and in the rear stood patient little
donkeys, ready saddled, for carrying the expected
visitors on a trip up to the village. We were just
about to blot the whole of Germany from our
minds, when my friend Alessio, shading his eyes
with his hand, suddenly observed that the steamer
which had just come in sight was not the usual
passenger steamer from Naples, but a larger and
faster boat. I looked at my watch, it was barely
three o'clock; I had hoped for at least another
hour's respite. Alessio was right; it was not the
usual boat that hove in sight. And now the Marina
began to wake up, and people came pouring in
from all sides. We saw the deputation rush down
the hill at full speed, with the chorus at its heels,
and last of all came the court poet, who surely dis-
approved as much as we did at the Princess's
anticipating her visit by a whole hour. The steamer
was certainly going at a greater speed than the

ordinary boat, and she also seemed to draw more water, as she backed farther out than usual from the harbour. The solemn moment was at hand; the deputation stood on the landing-stage in battle array, headed by the commercial traveller. We saw several people descend the ladder and step into a little boat, which rapidly made for the shore.

"Heil dir im Sieges Kranz!"

was now performed, and hardly had they got through the first verse when the boat pulled up alongside the little quay, and two ladies and a gentleman in uniform prepared to land. If they thought this would prove so easy a matter, they were mistaken—they were stopped short by the commercial traveller from Potsdam, who solemnly and warningly stretched out his right hand towards them, while with his left he drew a paper out of his trousers pocket. My old compassion for the Crown Princess rose anew, but what could I do for her? All hope of escape was at an end—

"Ich stehe hier auf Felsenstrand"—

but here there was a sudden silence. One of the ladies laughingly bent forward to say a few words to the gentleman in uniform, who quietly informed the deputation that these two ladies of the Princess's suite were anxious to make an excursion up to the village, while the Princess herself, who had remained on board, would sail round the island. At that very moment we saw the steamer veer round and make for the western side of the island.

Utterly dumbfounded, the deputation held a council of war as to the best course to be pursued. It was evident that the steamer had gone to make "il giro" (*i.e.,* the usual round of the island), to return finally to the Grande Marina, the only real landing-place which Capri possesses. True that a sort of harbour also exists on the south side at the Piccola Marina, but it has fallen into disuse, and the road hence into the village is very rough. They therefore decided to await the steamer's return where they were; more than an hour it would scarcely take. The deputation sank dejectedly down upon some upturned boats, but the poet remained standing for fear of creasing his dress-coat (fancy wearing a dress-coat and top-hat in Capri!). And he ran no chance of freezing, I can tell you, as he stood there in his sun-bath. The hour dragged wearily along, but still no sign of the steamer. They had waited for nearly two hours, when a fisherman phlegmatically observed that as far as he could make out the steamer had gone to the Piccola Marina, for he had rowed past just as the jolly-boat set out from the steamer, and some one on the captain's bridge had asked him how many feet of water they might count upon at the Piccola Marina. Up flew the deputation as if stung by an asp, and disappeared in a cloud of dust on the Capri road.

We dawdled about the Marina for some time longer, but finally we also wandered up to Capri not by the broad carriage-road, but climbing the old path which joins the Anacapri road at some distance from the village, thus avoiding the piazza altogether.

It was as warm as a summer's day, and we lay down by the roadside to rest in the high grass. We talked politics by way of exception. My friend D—— is an Alsatian; he had been through the Franco-German war, and was anything but tender towards the Germans, and neither was I, for reasons of my own. But we were generous enemies, and we agreed that we were very sorry for the Crown Princess, however German she might be.

And thus I came to speak of my nocturnal adventure with the commercial traveller; and no one being within earshot, it is just possible that we cracked a joke or two at the poet's expense. I remember that we tried to steer him safely through his poem, and lay there roaring with laughter, composing some extra verses to his unfinished inspiration. My old dog lay beside me in the grass; he did his best to follow us in our poetical flights, but the heat had made him somewhat indifferent to literary pursuits, and he never succeeded in keeping more than one eye open at a time. From out the ivy covering the old stone wall

behind us a little quick-tailed lizard peeped every
now and then to warm itself in the sun. Whenever
you catch sight of one of these little lizards you
should whistle softly; the graceful little animal will
then stand still, gazing wonderingly around with
her bright eyes to see from whence the sound pro-
ceeds. She is so frightened that you can see her
heart beat in her brilliant green breast, but she is
so curious and so fond of music—and there is so
little music to be heard inside the old stone wall!
You only have to keep quite quiet to see her emerge
from her hiding-place and settle down to listen
attentively. Something rather sentimental is what
pleases her best; she likes Verdi, and I often start
with Traviata when I give concerts for lizards. I
am so fond of music myself, and maybe that is the
reason why I try to be kind to these small music-
lovers. That any one can have the heart to take the
pretty, graceful little lizards captive is more than
I can understand; they belong to an old Italian
wall as much as the ivy and the sunshine. But there
is a German in Albergo Pagano who does nothing
but go about hunting lizards; he shuts them up in
a cigar-box, which he opens every now and then
to gaze like another Gulliver upon his Lilliputian
captives. We are deadly enemies, he and I, for once
I opened his cigar-box and set all his lizards free.

Suddenly Tappio gave a growl. We looked up,
and to our great astonishment we saw two ladies

standing in front of us, and behind them stood a gentleman in black, staring fixedly into space. We had not heard them come up, so that they must have been standing there while D—— and I were busy finishing off the commercial traveller's poem. We looked at each other in consternation, but there was evidently nothing to fear; it was not difficult to see that they were English, and not likely to have understood one word of what we had been talking about. One of the ladies was middle-aged, rather stout, and wore a grey travelling-dress while the other was a very smart young lady, whom we thought very good-looking indeed. They stood there gazing out over the Marina, and on looking in the same direction we saw that the Princess's steamer had returned from its "giro" round the island, and had anchored beside the Naples boat. Our discomfiture was complete upon the younger of the ladies turning round to ask us in perfect French how long it would take them to get to the village. D——, who was lying nearest them, answered it would hardly take ten minutes.

"Is it necessary to go through the village in order to reach the beach?" said she, pointing towards the Marina.

"Yes," answered D——, "it is necessary to do so."

Here Tappio stretched himself and stared yawningly at them.

"What a beautiful dog!" I heard the elder lady say to her companion in English. I at once discovered her to be a lady of great distinction and exceptional taste, and I immediately felt a desire to show her some politeness. I could not hit upon anything better to tell her than that she had chosen an unfortunate day for coming to Capri, the island having fallen a prey to the barbarians for the whole day. I told her that the Crown Princess of Germany was actually on the island, and that, pursued by a deputation and a commercial traveller, she had just now been caught on the Piccola Marina and carried off to the piazza. I added that all our sympathies followed the Princess. I noticed a rather peculiar expression on the younger lady's face as I delivered myself of these remarks, but the elder listened to all I said with a scarcely perceptible smile over her eyes.

"We are anxious to reach the harbour as soon as possible," said she; "we have been absent longer than we intended."

"There is a short cut down to the Marina," answered I, politely; "we have just come up that way ourselves. But I am afraid it is rather too rough a road for you, madam."

"Will it lead us straight down there?" said she, pointing to the harbour where both steamers lay at anchor.

"Oh dear, yes!"

"And without obliging us to enter the village?"

"Without obliging you to enter the village," answered I.

She exchanged a few words with the younger lady, and then said in a decided, abrupt sort of way, "Be kind enough to show us the way."

Yes, that was easy enough, and I led them down to the Marina. Conversation rather languished on the way. I had come across two singularly reticent ladies, and had it not been for my repeated efforts it would have died altogether. Every now and then the younger lady smiled to herself, which made me fear I had said something stupid. I have never been much of a society man, and it is not so easy a matter to entertain two entirely strange ladies.

Upon reaching the wider part of the road I pointed towards the Marina at their feet, and told them that they could not possibly go wrong now. We saw two officers walking up and down the landing-stage, whereupon I told the ladies that, were they desirous of seeing the Crown Princess, they had only to wait there a moment or two; she was bound to arrive soon with her tormentors at her heels. But this, they said, they did not care about, and then they kindly wished me good-bye.

Hardly had I begun to retrace my steps when two lackeys came running down the road; I had barely time to move to one side before they were yards beyond me. They were immediately followed by a long, gaunt individual with very thin legs and a very big moustache—*ma foi!* if not a German officer, remarkably like one at all events. He in his turn was succeeded by a fat, fussy little person, who literally threw himself into my arms; he held his gold-laced hat in one hand, while with the other he wiped the perspiration from his forehead; he stammered an apology, and then rolled off again like a ball down the hill. Most extraordinary, thought I to myself, the number of people on this footpath to-day, considering that as a rule one never meets a soul here!

D—— still lay on the Anacapri road waiting for me; neither of us cared to return to Capri just then, and we finally made up our minds to walk up to Anacapri and greet *la bella Margherita,* and wait there till the island should be restored to calm. We sat for a while under the pergola and drank a glass of vino blanco, and then we slowly sauntered down to Capri along the beautiful road, the whole of the myrtle-covered mountain slope at our feet. When passing beneath Barbarossa's ruined castle we glanced towards the Marina and saw to our relief that both steamers had taken their departure. Genuine Capriotes always witness the departure of the steamer with a certain satisfaction; they like to keep their beloved Capri to themselves, and the crowd of noisy strangers only disturbs the harmony of the dreamy little island.

It was very nearly dark by the time we reached the village. The piazza was quite deserted; from the shop-window of Nicolino, barber and bleeder, hung the tricoloured flag waving sadly in the wind, whilst perched upon the triumphal arch the cardboard eagle sat aloft gnawing gloomily at his "Willkommen."

Upon reaching the hotel we found that every one was seated at table, but an unusual silence prevailed. We withdrew to our little table and tried to look as innocent as possible. At dessert there arose a frightful dispute at the big table as to whose was the fault of a certain calamity which apparently had happened to them during the day. I thought I heard a murmur going round about an idiot who had been seen accompanying two ladies down a short cut to the Marina, but I never got to know who he was. Ah well! neither D—— nor I care to tell you more about this story. If we behaved badly I have already been sufficiently punished. Here I sit far from my beloved island in fog and gloom, whilst the commercial traveller, for aught I know, is perhaps still enjoying himself at Capri, and still entertaining the cocks of Pagano with—

"Ich stehe hier auf Felsenstrand!"

CHAPTER XI

THE DOGS IN CAPRI

The Dogs in Capri

AN INTERIOR

LIKE the ancient Romans, the Capri dogs devote
the greater part of their day to public life. The
piazza is their forum, and it is there they write
their history. When Don Antonio opens the
doors of his *osteria,* and Don Nicolino, barber and
bleeder, steps out of his *salone,* Capri begins a new
day. From all sides the dogs then come gravely
walking forth—the doctor's, the tobacconist's, the
secretary's, Don Archangelo's, Don Pietro's, etc.,
etc., and, after a greeting in accordance with nature's prescribed ceremonial, they seat themselves
upon the piazza to meditate. Don Antonio places
a couple of chairs in front of his café, and whilst
some of them accept the invitation to lean against
them, others prefer the steps leading up to the
church, or that comfortable corner by the campanile, to whose clock generations have listened
with ever-increasing astonishment where, indomi-

table as the sun, it presses forward on its own path, but alas! not that of the sun.

After a while the dogs of Hôtel Pagano make their appearance. They get up later than the others, for they eat a terribly solid dinner. They all descend from the venerable old "Timberio" [1] Pagano, who walks a little behind the rest of his family. Timberio has a cataract in one eye, but the other eye looks out upon life with immovable calm. The Pagano dog-family has always ranked amongst the very first in Capri, and now, since one of their masters, Manfredo, was made Sindaco, they have still further accentuated that reserved bearing which they always knew how to maintain towards the lower orders. They usually form a circle of themselves and some of the Liberal dogs in the Municipal Portico. The Conservative dogs, who were beaten in the last election when the Liberal candidate, Manfredo Pagano, became Sindaco, cluster together in a hostile minority on the other side of the piazza by the steps leading up to the church. Now and then they take a look inside the church, and seat themselves down by the door with the greatest decorum, like humble publicans, whilst the Mass is said in the chancel or the "Figlie di Maria" intone the Litany with half-singing voices.

[1] I write here as I talk here—not Italian but Capri dialect. The old emperor, who lived on the island for eleven years, is never called Tiberio here, but "Timberio."

About ten o'clock Il Cacciatore's [1] two dogs, mother and son, make their appearance. They walk without hesitation straight into Don Antonio's wineshop. They were born upon the island, but they have received an English education, and they well know the taste of a leg of mutton or a piece of roast beef. Don Antonio's dogs have also a certain idea of these things, and after several generations a vague Anglicism still survives amongst them from the time when Don Antonio was steward on board an English steamboat. The German dogs never enter this place; in spite of all Bismarck's efforts to win Don Antonio over to the triple alliance, they are not well looked upon there, their permanent headquarters are still at Morgano's "Zum Hiddigeigei," whence one can hear them barking and yelping till late at night.

The morning passes in calm *dolce far niente* as a preparation for the exertions of the day. Seldom has anything happened since they met here yesterday, seldom is there the slightest indication that the new day will bring in its train any change in the imperturbable harmony of their *status quo*. A contemplative calm is stamped upon their faces,

[1] Our friend, old Mr G——, for fifteen years the delight and ornament of the Piazza of Capri, always cheerful, always thirsty, a great destroyer of quails and wine bottles, now at last gone to rest in the quiet little field outside the town of Capri, where the sombre green of some laurel and cypress-trees stands out between the waving branches of his favourite plant, the vine. Old Spadaro is still alive, and will tell you all about his lamented master.

an Arcadian peace rules their whole existence. And yet this peace hovers over a volcano, like the summer which brightens the slopes of Vesuvius away on the far horizon. Now and then the thunder growls from the depths of Timberio Pagano's broad breast when Hôtel Quisisana's shaggy black guardian comes too near him. Seated on each side of the *farmacia* door the two rival doctors' four-footed assistants stick out their tongues at each other on the sly, and often enough do the dogs of Don Nicolino and Don Chichillo (the new barber) fall upon each other, so that tufts of hair fly around. Animosity, however, is soon forgotten, and, like the rippling waves against the old emperor's bath palace below, the hours come and go in rhythmic monotony.

They watch the girls as they stride past with mighty Tufa stones on their well-poised heads, like the Caryatides of the Erechtheum; they watch the Marina fishermen bringing up for sale in baskets the night's haul of golden *Triglie* and great *Scurmi,* of bright-coloured mussels from some rocky reef, or perhaps a coral-spun old Roman amphora dragged up by the deep *Palamido* nets from out of its thousand-year-old hiding-place at the bottom of the sea.

Sometimes their longing for activity is roused, and they slowly cross the piazza to the corner of the Anacapri road to gaze dreamily upon the

bustling life in front of the stables, where caval-
cades of *forestieri* are waiting impatiently whilst
saddles are laid upon the donkey's bleeding backs,
and rusty bits are stuffed into their sore mouths.
"Aaaaah! Aaaaah! Avanti!!" Off, little donkeys,
for Monte Solaro, one hour and a half's stiff
climbing with the happy tourists! Yes, the road
is beautiful, winding up along the side of the
mountain, clad with myrtle and broom. The view
widens more and more—"Aaaaaah! Aaaaaaaah!!"
One more climb, and the vineyards and olive woods
lie deep under your feet, and over your head rise
steep cliffs as wild in their mighty desolation as
the Via Mala of the Alps; and Barbarossa's half-
crumbling castle riveted fast upon the edge of the
precipice. Beyond gleams the gulf girdled by the
immortal beauty of the shore, and from Posilipo's
pine-crowned point, island after island floats away
towards the blue distance of the Mediterranean—
"wunderbar! kolossal!!"

Under the saddle it burns like fire, and the mouth
is so sore with the incessant tugging at the heavy
bridle; but courage, little donkey! Up above upon
the heights lives Padre Anselmo in his hermit
chapel, and he has good wine for thirsty throats!

Other dogs who do not get as far as the donkey-
stand lean thoughtfully against the parapet of the
piazza, where some lounging sailors look out over
the gulf. The eyes wander towards the gleaming

outline of Naples, and the mighty silhouette of Vesuvius, or absently follow the direction of some outstretched hand pointing towards Capo Sorrento, whence can be seen the steamboat on its way to Capri. And here come the two blind old men, Fenocchio and Giovanni, groping their way across the piazza to their usual corner at the edge of the path, where the hum of thousands of gay tourists has rustled by them, where they have sat for so many years with their old fisher-caps in outstretched hands, and their vacant eyes staring into their eternal night of gleaming sunshine: "Date u soldo Eccellenza al povero cieco! La Madonna vi accompagna!"

Up on the piazza the dogs are beginning to awake, and in scattered groups they wander across to the parapet to stare at the steamboat which glides past in the blue water on its way to the grotto. It is time to start down to the Marina to greet the new arrivals. Quisisana's, Pagano's, and Hôtel de France's dogs solemnly escort their respective porters to the arched entrance of the piazza with its Bourbon coat-of-arms still enthroned above it. Small ready-saddled donkeys also clatter patiently down the old stairway to the Marina, and with loud cracks of the whip Felicello's coachmen rattle down the new carriage-road. From the piazza above, they watch the steamer anchoring outside the harbour. and the small boats landing the pas-

sengers. A faint interest lights up the passive faces
of the lookers-on when the first strangers reach the
piazza. But alas! always the same invariable types,
always the same colossal matron on the same slender
little donkey, always the same correct "misses" in
Felicello's landau; always the same fiery-red noisy
Germans, wrangling over prices with the girls who
have dragged their boxes up the height to the town.
Seldom are there any dogs amongst the arrivals,
seldom does any occasion whatever arise for inter-
ference in one way or another—passivity, nothing
but passivity!

Now the hotel bells ring for luncheon, and they
one and all wander home. The processes of digestion
are carried out, according to correct physiological
laws undisturbed by any brain-work, and the afternoon is passed in a siesta on some loggia, whilst the
sun's rays slowly climb the Anacapri cliff, and long
shadows begin to glide down Monte Solaro's slopes
towards the town. The air is cool and refreshing,
and they prepare to resume public life on the piazza.
The second event of the day is at hand. The post
arrives. Don Peppino Pagano (postmaster) solemnly shuts his office door, and the loiterers wait
with interest whilst the postbag is being opened
inside. Always the same disappointment—no letters
for them, all the letters and newspapers are for the
foreigners in the hotels! Sometimes they get hold
of a *Corriere di Napoli* or a *Pungolo,* and then they

disappear into some corner by themselves to make people believe that they can read; but after they have devoured the whole newspaper they are none the wiser for it. So they become drowsy again, and wander a few times round the piazza, past Don Antonio's *osteria* with the faded photographs and dried-up biscuits in the window, and a few unconscious philosophers meditating inside; past Il Salone, where the flies keep watch over Don Nicolino's dreams; past La Farmacia, where the morphia of idleness soothes Don Petruccio's ideas to rest; past the stable where the donkeys are pushed into their dark holes after the strangers have returned from their expedition. They look out over the gulf where Ischia blushes in the fading sunlight, while dark-blue twilight falls around Vesuvius. The day's session draws to an end, and the piazza is becoming deserted. Up in the campanile a terrible commotion amongst the cogs and wheels suddenly breaks forth, and at last the old machinery loses its temper altogether, and, getting hold of a rusty hammer, begins to beat with all its might on some unwilling bells: "Ventiquattro ore," yawns Don Nicolino, shutting up his *salone;* "Ventiquattro ore," say the flies, and go to sleep amongst the brushes and combs; "Ventiquattro ore," say the dogs, and go home with the feeling of having performed their duty, to gather strength for the next

day's toil by twelve or fourteen hours' dreamless
sleep.

Then the church bells ring out the Ave Maria,
and the day sinks into the sea.

So passes day after day, each like the other, as
the beads of the rosaries which glide between the
fingers of the "Figlie di Maria" inside the church.
Each morning brings together the citizens for social
duty on the piazza—each evening the campanile
exhorts them to go to rest.

Under the walls of the houses the shadows begin
to shorten, and the paving-stones of the piazza get
hotter and hotter in the sun-bath. Uneasy dreams
now disturb the peace of the siesta, and Capri is
seized with an irresistible desire to scratch itself.
Don Antonio spreads the awning before his wineshop, and the questions of the day are oftener and
oftener dealt with under its protecting shade. They
linger later on the piazza in the warm evenings, and
with nose in the air they sit for long hours on the
parapet looking out over the gulf towards Vesuvius, whose mighty smoke-cloud slowly spreads over
the mainland—the wind is south, all is as it should
be! And, with apprehensive thoughts of fatigues to
come, they troop home to their much-needed repose.

The piazza is quite empty, now and then a short
bark is heard from some wineshop, or a howling
"Potz Donner Wetter!" from Hiddigeigei's beer-

house; then everything is still, and only the old watchman in the campanile counts aloud the hours of the night in a sonorous brazen voice to keep himself awake. Still for a while the white town gleams out amongst the cliffs, then it becomes quite dark, and Capri's isle sinks into the gloom of night.

But lo! the moon already climbs Sorrento's mountain, and the veil of twilight glides down Monte Solaro's heights, over shimmering olive woods, over orange and myrtle groves, and vanishes amid the waves of the gulf. Night dreams a beautiful dream, and mysteriously the siren's moonlit island rises out of the dark sea. A gentle south wind breathes over the water, murmurs amidst the half-slumbering waves, flies fragrantly over orange-trees in blossom, and playfully rocks the tender vine branches. Jubilant voices call out from the sea, louder and louder they sound in the stillness of the night, and the wanderer on Monte Solaro hears the rustling of wings in the moonlight space above.

When Capri awakes the next morning, everyone knows that the wild geese have passed. Spring has come, and the shooting season has begun! From early morning the piazza is full of dogs. The *dolce far niente* of everyday life is over, a certain energy animates their dull features, and the reflection of an idea lights up the contemplative gloom of their eyes.

In front of Maria Vacca's butcher-shop hangs a dead quail, and outside Don Antonio's *osteria* stand guns in long rows, and upon the chairs lie great gamebags and powder-horns. Il Cacciatore has been in the wineshop since sunrise, in colossal shooting-boots and cartridge-belt round his waist. Woe to the quail which may now appear in Maria Vacca's shop! It vanishes at once into Il Cacciatore's gamebag. Inside the Municipal Portico a younger generation listens to old Timberio Pagano's shooting stories of the days of his youth, when many thousand quails were caught in a day, and up on the church steps the clericals think sadly of that period of vanished splendour when Capri had its own bishop, whose maintenance was paid by the quail harvest—"Vescovo delle quaglie" [1] as he was called in Rome. Excitement increases as the hours pass, and when at last the bells of the campanile announce that the first day's shooting is over, each one goes to his home to gather strength for the next day's exertions. Once again darkness falls upon the island, and Capri sleeps the sleep of the just.

On tired wings swarms of birds fly over the sea. Thousands have fallen on Africa's coasts, where they assembled for their long journey, thousands have sunk exhausted amidst the waves, thousands will die on the rocky island which glimmers from

---

[1] Quail bishop. Capri no longer owns a bishop, but the quail harvest still forms one, and perhaps the most important item of the island's revenue.

afar in the darkness. Sheltered by the last hour of
gloom they approach the island and silently swoop
down upon its steep coast, upon the heights by Villa
di Tiberio, where the hermit watches behind his
snares; amongst the cliffs of Mitromania and the
Piccola Marina, where nets are spread to catch their
wings; upon the headlands of Limbo and Punta di
Carena, where the Capri dogs, stealthy as cats,
sneak round after their prey. When day dawns over
Monte Solaro, and its first rays stream, even as
they did two thousand years ago, in sacred fire upon
the old sun-god's crumbling altar in the grotto
of Mitromania,[1] hundreds of birds, quails, wood-
pigeons, larks, thrushes, flutter in the nets around,
and hundreds of others bleed to death amongst
the cliffs—but what cares the sun for that! What
matters it to the sun that the darkness he disperses
conceals a multitude of worn-out birds from rapacious eyes, that to-day death stalks from cliff to
cliff along the track shown by his gleaming light:

> "So che Natura ĕ sorda,
> Che miserar non sa;
> Che non del Ben sollecita
> Fu, ma dell 'esser solo." [2]

Upon the heights of Monte Salaro sits Il Caccia-

---

[1] Few strangers visit the grotto of Mitromania, the name of which
may be derived from *Magnum Mitrae Antrum*. It faces east, and the
first rays of the sun light up its mysterious gloom. One knows from
excavations made here that once upon a time, the old, yet ever young
sun-god was worshipped in this cave.

[2] Leopardi.

tore, armed to the teeth, looking with the eye of a
conqueror over the field of battle below. The day
has been a hot one, Il Cacciatore has fired some
hundred shots in different directions. At his feet
lie his two dogs, mother and son, and behind him
sits Spadaro with an extra gun in his hands and an
enormous gamebag over his shoulder. Now and then
mother and son give little yelps and wag their tails,
pursuing in their dreams an escaping bird, now and
then Il Cacciatore's hand fumbles after his trusty
gun to bring down an imaginary quail or pigeon,
now and then Spadaro seems to stuff some new
booty into his vast bag. Deeper and deeper grows
the silence over Monte Solaro. Down at their feet
the three rocks of Faraglione shine in purple and
gold, and the glow of the sinking sun falls on the
waves of the gulf. From the town of Capri hotel
bells ring for dinner. A fragrant hallucination of
quail-pie tickles Il Cacciatore's nostrils, and from
under his half-shut eyelids the whole gulf assumes
a tantalising resemblance to a sea of pure *Capri
rosso*—that purple hue which already old Homer
likened to red wine—whilst Spadaro's more modest
imagination hears the macaroni splutter and boil
in the murmur of the waves against the cliff below,
and sees the purple glow of the evening sun pour
masses of *pumaroli*[1] sauce over it.

[1] *Pumaroli-pomidoro, i.e.,* tomato, the Southern Italians' favourite
fruit, the most important ingredient in everything he eats, sweetening
the monotony of his macaroni.

Suddenly Il Cacciatore wakes up, rubs his eyes and looks dreamily around, and Spadaro investigates the bag with amazement, where only a single little lark, which was on its way to give spring concerts in the North, sleeps his last sleep. "Hallo! Spadaro! Andiamonci!" [1] The dogs wake up by degrees, and the caravan starts slowly on its way towards Capri. Tired by the day's toil, at last they reach the piazza and its friendly wineshop, where Il Cacciatore sits down to rest, whilst Spadaro and the dogs carry home the lark in triumph.

So pass the weeks of the shooting season in continued exertions. Every morning before daybreak they start off to try and capture spring in its flight, every evening they meet on the piazza to rest, and often enough do we assemble round our friend Il Cacciatore's hospitable table to partake of a magnificent quail-pie, such as only he can put before us.

But although the ranks are thinned, the March of The Ten Thousand still advances victoriously. Soon the larks sing over the frosty fields in the distant North, soon the swallows twitter under the eaves of the far-off little cottage, which has lain so long half-buried in the snow, and the quails sound their monotonous note in the soft spring evenings.

The shooting season is over, and the Capri dogs sit blankly upon the piazza, staring out over the

[1] "Let us be off."

gulf in the direction the bird flew when he escaped from their hands. Higher and higher the sacred fire flames each morning upon the sun-god's altar down in Mitromania's grotto, brighter and brighter the Faraglioni rocks gleam each evening with purple and gold, with a still ruddier glow the wine-hue of the gulf fascinates Il Cacciatore's retina. Silently the Liberal dogs ponder over the burning questions of the day, and, panting, the Clericals listen from their sunny church steps to the prophecies of the fires of *Il purgatorio,* which the priests proclaim every Sunday inside the cool church. Public life ceases by degrees, and it seems as if a reaction sets in after the excitement of the shooting season. Certainly the arrival of the steamer is still watched from the piazza, and with one eye open they gaze at the few foreigners who wander up to the piazza, with outspread sketching-umbrellas and easel and colour-box on a boy's head. True, they still assemble in front of the closed door of the post-office to await the opening of the post-bag, but interest in political life has slackened, and their hope of letters has become a quiet resignation. Inside the *farmacia* the drugs ferment in their pots, and in Don Nicolino's *salone* living frescoes of flies adorn the walls. About the slopes of Monte Solaro the Sirocco hangs in heavy clouds, and an irresistible drowsiness settles down upon the piazza. Capri enters into its summer torpor.

When it awakes the sun has subdued his fire, and the table stands ready spread for the lords of creation to seat themselves and feast, and for the dogs to gather up the fragments that remain. From the *pergola* over their heads hang grapes in heavy clusters, and amidst the shade of the orange-groves peep out juicy figs and red-checked peaches. Then comes the Bacchanalia of the vintage, with song and jest and maiden's bright eyes looking out from under huge baskets of grapes, and naked feet freeing the slumbering butterfly of wine from its crushed chrysalis.

Over the piazza a cooling sea-breeze blows now and again, and Capri takes a refreshing bath of autumnal rain to wash away the heat and dust of summer. The dogs save themselves in time from the vivacity of the unknown element, but millions of obscure lives are drowned in the streams which force their way like a deluge over the bloody battle-field of summer, whilst the survivors find their Ararat amongst the brushes in Don Nicolino's *salone*.

The mist of unconsciousness is gradually lifted from the dogs' brains, and waking dreams of activity and strength stare out from their half-shut eyes. Don Nicolino smilingly dusts the halo of flies from his portrait, and, deep in thought, Don Petruccio composes a new elixir of life from

summer's *mixtum compositum*. Fenocchio and
Giovanni seat themselves again in their corner to
wash a little copper out of the tourist stream, and
on trembling legs the small donkeys once more
unload numbers of *forestieri* in the piazza. From
Vesuvius the smoke falls in long cloud-streamers
over the gulf, and upon the wings of the Tramon-
tana (the north wind), summer flies home again
after her wedding-trip to the North. In vain do
the Capriotes spread their nets once more round
the shores of the island; in vain do the dogs lie in
wait amongst the rocks; in vain does Il Cacciatore
sit in full armour on the heights of Monte Solaro
and shoot off his cartridges after the fugitive—
summer passes by.

With drooping tails the dogs sit huddled together
upon the stones of their piazza, thinking with sorrow of their departed summer idyll. From snow-
covered Apennines, winter comes sailing in his
foam-hidden dragon-ship over the uneasy waters
of the gulf. The storm thunders amidst the ruins
of the old watch-tower, whose alarm-bell [1] has been
silent for so long, and amongst the foaming
breakers the mad Viking boards Capri's cliffs.
Strong as a whirlwind he cuts in pieces the pergola
garlands which were left hanging after autumn's

[1] The alarm-bell used to be rung from the old tower to warn the
shores of the gulf of the approach of pirates.

Bacchanalian feast, and, brutal as a savage, he tears asunder the leaf-woven chiton which clothed the Dryad of the grove.

But down in Mitromania's grotto the sacred fire flames as of old upon the Persian god's altar, and tenderly the God of Day spreads his shining shield over his beloved island and bids the barbarian from the North go to sea again. So he departs, the rough Viking, his errand unaccomplished, without having robbed a single rose from the maiden's sun-warmed cheek, without having stolen a single golden fruit from the everlasting green of the orange groves. And scarcely has he turned his back on the island before tiny fearless violets peep carefully out from among the hillocks, and narcissus and rosemary clamber high up on the steep cliffs to see whither the harsh Northerner has gone, and soon a whole flock of flower children come and set themselves down to play at summer in the grass.

Upon the piazza the dogs sit as before in sunny contemplation. The cycle of their life's emotions has been run through, and they begin to turn over anew the blank pages of their history, page after page, in unvarying sequence. Day follows day and year follows year, and soon old age comes and scatters some white almond blossom upon their heads. The buoyant delights of the senses are benumbed, youth's far-flying thought has broken its wings against the four walls of the piazza, and like tame ducks the dogs trot round and round their enclosed space, from Don Antonio's wineshop to Felicello's donkey-stand, from Don Nicolino's *salone* to Don Petruccio's *farmacia*. Now and again the free cry of the passing wild geese high over their heads reaches the piazza, the buoyancy of youth wakes afresh in them, and they sluggishly tramp along towards the Anacapri road as far as their heavy limbs can carry them. Now and again a faint echo from some world's revolution trembles on their tympanums through Don Peppino's post-office, and they look away in dreaming peace to the white town of Naples, the noise of whose human life is lost amidst the murmur of the waves, or away to the old revolutionist Vesuvius, whose threatening wrath will never reach their Eden.

So they sit on their piazza, staring out upon the river of time as it flows past them. They still sit there staring for a few more years to come, then they move no more—they have become hypnotised. The struggle for existence has ceased, and imperceptibly they sink into Buddha's Nirvâna, unconscious, painless, inebriate with the sun.

CHAPTER XII

SŒUR PHILOMÈNE

Sœur Philomène

THEY were both serving at the big Paris hospital.
She was a sister of charity, and he was reading
for his examination. She wore the white habit of
the Sisters of St. Augustin; but the novice's cap
still framed her delicate face, so young for all the
misery that surrounded her. No one knew whence
she came; she was "Sœur Philomène," that was all.
More than one of the young doctors had tried their
best to find out something about her, but the only
person who knew was the Mother Superior, who
always maintained a mysterious silence whenever
the name of the young sister of charity was mentioned.

It was always Sœur Philomène who at the morning round could report as to how a patient of the
ward had passed the night; it was always she who
knew best how to set the pillow right under the
weary head of the poor sufferer, restless and fretful
with his pain; it was always she who knew how to
speak the words of hope when the operation was
at hand and courage failed.

When the night-bell rang, and the doctor on
duty, sleepy and irritable, came up to see what was
the matter, it was always she who was there first,
bending over the bed, putting the bandage straight
with soft hands, or soothing with gentle words the
anguish of the long night.

One evening a boy who had been found lying
unconscious in the street was brought in from the
police station. He was bleeding from an ugly
wound in the head, and was quite stiff with cold.
He was a child of the poor, and only some thin,
ragged clothes protected his frail little body against
the cold winter's night. After his head had been
bandaged Sœur Philomène undressed him quickly,
and laid him in the warmed bed. He remained unconscious for some time, and then began to moan,
and tried to raise his hand to his head. Soon he
opened his eyes—large, wondering, child eyes—
and he looked at the white curtains round his bed
and across the dimly lighted ward. Presently the
half-thawed little fingers began to pick at the
counterpane, and then both hands groped about in
the bed as though in search of something. He became quieter after he had got hold of a tiny little
fiddle which had been found with him, and which
constituted the whole of his outfit. Clutching it
tightly he suddenly raised himself from the bed as
if he wanted to escape. The homeless little fellow,
accustomed to be turned away from every one's

door, probably thought that there was danger ahead, and now that he had found his fiddle his awakening consciousness warned him that he had better be off. But his head was too heavy, and he fell back again on the pillow. At the same moment he caught sight of the doctor who stood at the head of his bed, and with wide-open, suspicious eyes he stared at his blood-stained apron. The doctor saw that he was frightened and stepped back. But when Sœur Philomène at the same time bent over him, he became calmer, and looked her straight in the eyes with an expression both of curiosity and confidence.

The doctor went down to his room again. He was just then at that period of a young physician's life when he considers it rather the thing to show no feelings of compassion for the sick, when he tries hard to look callous and imperturbable; when the sick are mere illustrations in his medical hand-books, and the dead so many corpses which the anatomist scrutinises with the eyes of a connoisseur. . . .

The doctor thought he did not care in the very least what happened to the poor little waif up in the Salle St. Paul.

But after a while it struck him that it might be as well to go and see how the boy was getting on, and if the hæmorrhage had quite ceased. On the stairs he stopped short and said to himself that there was really nothing more for him to do up there that night, and that the boy had much better be left in peace. But he went up all the same. The last round for the night had been made, and everything was quite quiet in the ward. He went silently up to the newcomer's bed. Sœur Philomène was still sitting there; the homeless little musician was fast asleep with one arm round her neck, and his fiddle in his other hand.

Next morning he found out why he had not been able to resist his impulse to go and have a look at the boy during the night. Nobody knew where the lad came from, and his only answer to all the questions put to him was to stare at the professor and the students who stood round his bed. Just as an enterprising assistant was writing upon the slate over his bed, *Commotion cérébrale, perte de la parole,* the little fellow stuck his thumb into his mouth, winked with his eye, and gave a loud click with his tongue, to every one's amazement. And there was one by his bedside who understood; he knew the sign well from the crowds of boys on the Mergellina and Santa Lucia. "Tu sei Italiano?" he asked him.

"Si Signore, vengo da Napoli!" replied the little lazzarone. He was not in the least dumb, only frightened at all these strange people and their foreign language.

The boy had made a good friend for himself, a friend who was truly glad to look after him.

The boy's story was the usual one. He came from one of the mountain villages round Monte Cassino, and had begun life by wandering about the streets of Naples with his fiddle under his arm to earn his bread. From thence he had been taken to Paris on speculation.[1]

The boy had arrived in Paris only a few days ago, but had lost his way, and had wandered about in the streets till, exhausted with cold and hunger, he had fainted, and had been picked up by the police.

But the winter's night had been too cold for the ragged little Southerner. As the day wore on he began to cough; in the evening he was in a high fever, and the following morning there stood on the slate over his bed *Pneumonie double*—and this time, alas! the diagnosis was right enough.

During three nights Sœur Philomène watched over the poor little musician, and on the fourth day he died.

No one had taken any notice of him before; he belonged to nobody as long as he was alive, but once dead he belonged, according to the hospital rules, to the dissecting room. He had hardly grown

[1] Every year these white slave-traders come to Naples, choosing their victims from amongst the swarms of ragged street children, in order to send them to London or to Paris to make money out of them as street-singers or models.

cold before they came to carry him down to the
Anatomical Hall, where his frail little body was
soon to be cut to pieces by the dissecting knives of
the students. Sœur Philomène and the doctor were
standing by his bed, and their eyes met. He who
had been unable to save the life of his little friend,
now covered his face with the sheet, and beckoned
silently to the porter to delay his errand; and he
went down to see *Monsieur le Directeur*. He was
in the very good graces of the hospital authorities
just then, and with a little persuasion his request
was granted.

In the evening a small coffin was carried out of
the hospital gates; the funeral procession was not a
long one, only a Sister of Charity and a student.
The homeless little vagabond lay there in peace,
with his broken fiddle in his hand. And of all the
wealth of flowers which the luxury of the wintry
metropolis borrows each morning from the summer of the South, a handful of violets had found
its way into the coffin of the curly-headed little
musician, with a fragrant greeting from the land
of his birth, where his mother that same evening,
in the little church high up in the mountains, implored the Madonna to watch over her child wandering about all alone over the wide world.

.   .   .   .   .   .

Sœur Philomène remained as silent as before;

she never spoke except the few words necessitated
by the hospital service. But it seemed as if they
had something in common, the two friends of the
dead child. Sometimes it was she who had a special
protégé in the ward, and then he always managed
to get him placed amongst his patients. Sometimes
it was the doctor who was particularly interested in
some one, and then it seemed as though the gentle
sister was especially kind to him.

There were twelve Sisters of Charity in the
hospital. The Superior, *ma mère,* as they all called
her, had perhaps now and then made her little
attempts to convert the foreign assistant, for she
knew that he did not belong to that faith which
had bid her sacrifice her life under the veil of a
Sister of Charity. She had once asked him if they
never went to confession in his church, and never
lit the candles on the Blessed Virgin's altar, and
at his negative answer the old nun had shaken her
head compassionately but resignedly.

But for all that they were not bad friends, and
once he had even been allowed to play on the little
organ in the hospital chapel during High Mass,
when the old priest who usually played had been
taken ill.

By way of thanks he always stood up for the
Sisters of Charity in the daily discussions down in
the guard-room. *La laïcisation des hôpitaux* was
the burning question of the day, and all the self-

sacrificing devotion of the Sisters of Charity was powerless to put a stop to the agitation for their dismissal, and for the exclusion of all religion from the hospitals.

Every evening vespers were read in the chapel for those who were able to attend, and each sister read the prayers for the night in her own special ward. Often enough the doctor would remain for awhile up in the Salle St. Paul. When Sœur Philomène lit the candles on the little altar the moans and sighs would gradually cease, and a great silence would fall over the whole ward. Kneeling in the middle of the room the sister prayed with her clear voice for a peaceful night, and when she finished with the Ave Maria all the sick repeated it with her. Some were not able to follow her, and every now and again a trembling voice came lagging behind with the concluding words, "Priez pour nous pauvres pêcheurs, maintenant et à l'heure de notre mort!" And from some of the beds nothing could be heard but a feeble moan—but surely that, too, found its way along with the rest.

Sœur Philomène was looking so pale. One day she did not appear at the morning round, and it was said that she had had a hæmorrhage of the lungs during the night. But soon she was at her post again, as self-sacrificing as ever; night and day she was to be found in the wards helping and comforting as before, and never did she seem to give herself a moment's rest.

So the winter sped away. The windows stood open all day long, and spring entered the sombre wards, flying from bed to bed, and gently lifting the curtains, behind which pale sufferers lay waiting for their last chance—the summer.

Below in the courtyard the trees were in full leaf, and on the terrace the convalescents sat in long rows, warming themselves in the sun.

There was great festivity in the *Salle de Garde,* where all the comrades were drinking the health of the newly made doctor. There on the wall hung his old hospital blouse, stained and saturated with carbolic acid, and on the table, amongst heaps of books and papers, lay his old pipe, which had kept him company during so many nights of hard work. At the head of the table sat the doctor, the long-desired diploma in his pocket, and up in his student's room lay his knapsack ready packed for to-morrow's journey. Every one was talking at the top of his voice, and no one was listening. The doctor managed to slip out of the room unnoticed, and once more he walked up the well-known corridor leading to the Salle St. Paul. He stopped in the doorway, and he heard whispered from bed to bed, "La ronde de la sœur!" And there came Sœur Philomène with the night-lamp in her hand walking through the dim ward. He looked at the sad, pale face, and he felt how much he had learnt to care for the gentle sister, although he had hardly ever spoken a word to her. When she had finished her round he went up to bid her farewell. He was going far away, and would probably never see her again, but before he left he wanted to tell her how it grieved him to see her looking so pale and ill, and he begged her to consider that she was killing herself with her constant care of the sick. "I am happy," was all she answered. He forgot the severe rules of her Order, and held out his hand to bid her farewell, but she did not take it.

He was gone for a long time. One evening he stood again before the old hospital. It looked exactly the same, the sombre walls sheltered the same suffering and sorrow as before. It was just the hour when Sœur Philomène used to read the evening prayers up in the Salle St. Paul, and he went there. But the little altar had been knocked down, the crucifix was no more to be seen, Sœur Philomène was gone, all the dear sisters were gone. A student in the well-known hospital blouse came towards him—perhaps he would be able to tell him what he wanted to know.

"Ah! yes, the Sisters! It is long since they were turned out!"

"Just so, 'tis long since they were turned out."

"And the white-haired old chaplain, is he here still?"

"There is no chaplain here, there is no chapel, what would be the use of it! Maybe you were here before," said the student, eyeing the visitor with curiosity; "it must have been before my time."

"Yes, it must have been before your time." It must have been long, long ago thought he to himself, as he turned away, for he felt such a stranger amidst all these improvements. He lingered about the courtyard for awhile watching the light in the little window of his old room. Probably a new student was sitting there cramming for his examination—would that he might come further in the long history of human suffering than his predecessor in the courtyard under his window, for he never got further than the chapter on man's helplessness; and there he marked his book with a cross.

.   .   .   .   .   .

It was several years later. The doctor had left Paris for a short holiday, and had gone down to Naples to pay a visit to the land he loved so well. Altogether idle he was not, for idleness fosters hypochondria. He did not go in for much studying—but he was on his holiday after all. All the others were writing long dissertations on the cholera, but he wrote nothing, for he had nothing

to say. And the microbes—the famous microbes
which, small as they are, are nevertheless sufficient
to make many a doctor great—he did not trouble
himself much about them either. He did not feel
more inclined to examine them through the micro-
scope than to examine the far-away, glittering
stars of the night through the telescope. What
he saw with his eyes was enough. He saw with
sorrow how terribly the poor people suffered.

The cholera was on the wane, but the famine
grew worse and worse. He did not often go to
the cholera hospital, for those who were lying
there stood in no need of his help; better doctors
than he gave them their assistance, and charity
took care of their families as far as possible. One
evening, however, he went there, for he had
happened to hear that a Sister of Charity was
dying there.

In the corridor he met one of the doctors who,
in answer to his question, pointed to the door of one
of the private rooms—"Stadium algidum," said he,
and went on his way.[1]

The room was half dark, two Sisters of Charity
were kneeling in prayer, and on the bed lay Sœur
Philomène pale as death. She slowly opened her
eyes, and her glance fell straight on him as he stood
there at her side.

[1] The cholera characteristic, algid state, when the body has grown
cold.

"I knew you were here," she said. And this time she gave him her hand; but it was hers no longer, it belonged to life no more, it was already quite cold. Presently she seemed to fall asleep, she lay there quite quietly, save that she now and then opened her eyes and looked long and fixedly at those who surrounded her bed. Towards morning she began to shiver, and they folded her white habit round her. She was then quite cold, but they could see by her eyes that she was still conscious. Her lips moved as though to say something, but the power of speech had gone. The painful shadow over her forehead, which he knew so well, vanished more and more, for her eyes began to glow with a joy of which this world knows nothing. Then her soul took wing, and the peace of death fell over her face.

And those who stood round knew that she was happy.

CHAPTER XIII

WHEN TAPPIO WAS LOST

XIII

WHEN TAPPIO WAS LOST

IT HAD grown quite dark in Santa Maria del Carmine. Here and there the light of a wax candle fell upon some poor people, who had yet something to confide to the Mother of God; who yet wished to invoke her powerful help in some distress; yet wished to implore her to grant some peace to their anguished hearts.

Santa Maria del Carmine is the church of the poor, and the poor knew well that they now needed the Madonna's help more than ever. Some of them had timidly advanced as far as the miraculous crucifix, which human hands had been unable to destroy, and which had more power to protect them than San Gennaro himself, the patron saint of Naples.[1] Most of them had stopped in the side aisle, whilst some had not ventured further than the door, where,

---

[1] Here is what the sacristan will tell you about this crucifix. During the siege of Naples by Alfonso of Aragon in 1439, a bullet pierced the window above the high altar, and went whizzing through the air in the direction of the crucifix, but the image bowed its head and the bullet lodged in the wall. At the same moment in the besiegers' camp Alfonso's brother was struck by a bullet in the head, and fell to the ground mortally wounded.

with humble obeisance, they kissed the threshold of the Blessed Mother's sanctuary.

The bells rang out Ave Maria, and one after another rose, and, with a profound reverence, went away. The church was about to be closed, and I walked slowly down one of the aisles. At that moment a man entered the church; he fell upon his knees, and while his lips murmured fervent prayers he made the sign of the cross over and over again, and, as though in deepest despair, he bent down and struck his forehead against the marble floor.

The sacristan came to lock the door, the man rose, threw his cloak over his shoulder, and hurriedly left the church. Just as I passed the spot where he had been kneeling, my foot struck something, I bent down and picked up a long Calabrian dagger which lay on the floor. We two were the last to leave the church, and I caught him up in the piazza. He started as I handed him the knife, and with a rapid movement, he snatched it from me. His face was deathly pale, and there was a strange, uncanny gleam in his eye; I was so struck by his appearance that I could not help telling him that I had noticed him in the church, and that I felt sorry for him. He looked at me with knitted brows, and he muttered through his clenched teeth: "Cholera in casa!"

I told him that I happened to be a doctor, and, pointing to my instrument case under my arm, I offered him my assistance if he thought I could be of any use to him; but he shook his head and walked away.

I lingered on the piazza for a while, wondering whether after all it would not be best to go straight home to bed; I had been very busy the whole day, and had merely entered the quiet old church to have a little rest.

Just as I was walking off, I saw to my surprise the man with the cloak coming up to me.

"Siete forestiere?" [1] said he abruptly. I answered "yes."

"Non avete niente a fare con Il Municipio?" [2] said he.

"Niente affatto." [3]

"Volete venire con me?" [4] he said again.

Of course I wanted to go with him. We walked down Via Lavinaio, and turned into one of the slums behind the little church of San Matteo; for a while I knew more or less of my whereabouts, but soon I lost my bearings, and ere long I had not the slightest idea where we were. Once or twice I asked him the names of the streets, but he made no reply. It had become quite dark, and I wondered what o'clock it might be; but none of the people we came across looked as if they had a watch, although I must admit that several of them looked as if they

[1] "Are you a stranger?"
[2] "You have nothing to do with the municipal authorities?"
[3] "Nothing at all."
[4] "Will you come with me?"

would have liked to get hold of one. But nobody said an unkind word to us; once or twice it seemed to me that they made way for us, and I even thought I noticed a sort of greeting exchanged between some of them and my companion—that is to say, as far as I could see in the uncertain light of the little lamps which here and there lit up the Madonna's shrines.

We went through a vaulted passage, and emerged into a little alley so narrow that we could not walk abreast. All of a sudden my companion asked me if I knew where we were, and I answered him with perfect truth that I did not even know what quarter of the town we were in. Shortly afterwards we stopped before a miserable tumble-down house, and I heard him exchange a few words with somebody I could not see. What surprised me most was, that I could not understand a single word they said—I, who flattered myself upon speaking the Neapolitan dialect better than many Italians. A man came out from the house; we all three entered a pitch-dark passage, and I heard the door being bolted behind us. My companion took me by the hand, which was just as well, as I could not see a yard before me. We crossed a courtyard, and pulled up before a low hovel, from which a faint light glimmered through the closed shutters. I thought to myself it was only Naples and some melodramatic novels which could produce such an adventure as this promised to turn out: and certainly the man who now came forward to light us up the steps would have made a capital model for a brigand. More conversation between him and my companion, of which, notwithstanding my best endeavours, I understood nothing. I only managed to catch the word *misericordia* several times, from which I concluded that they were talking about our meeting in the church; I had gleaned from Cæsare that *misericordia* means "knife" in the language of the Camorra. The man raised the lantern to my face and examined me closely, but I could not make out how he liked my looks, for he did not say a word.

We were now standing before a half-open door, my companions crossed themselves, and we silently entered. It was the' usual sight; the mother lay prostrated before the image of the Madonna, wringing her hands in despair, and, close by, a couple of women were kneeling in fervent prayer. Crouching beside the fire sat an old woman, muttering to herself in a weird sing-song voice a string of incoherent words which sounded more like incantations than prayers; I heard afterwards that she was *la nonna* (grandmother), and was supposed not to be in her right mind.

There was no one near the bed.[1] I took the lan-

---

[1] The Neapolitan people are very reluctant to touch the dying unless it is absolutely necessary; they remain in the room, but always at a certain distance from the bed.

tern out of the hand of the man from Santa Maria
del Carmine, and the light fell upon a livid child-
face on the pillow; the strong man beside me shook,
and I felt that it was his child. The child had already begun to grow cold, and seemed quite unconscious. Surreptitiously, under the blanket, I gave
her an ether injection, which made her rally a little,
and although it was only momentary, it was enough
to soften the suspicious eyes around me. The little
girl began to moan, whereupon they all eagerly
crowded round the bed alternately watching her
and me. The mother who in her despair had not
even noticed our arrival, rose hastily the moment
the child began to groan, and half beside herself,
started to help me to rub her with the blanket.

The frictions proved useless, and the child was
sinking fast. I decided to make a certain intra-
venous injection I had been experimenting with of
late. Whilst I was preparing for the operation there
arose a heated discussion in the room. The opin-
ions were evidently divided, the majority inclined
towards "lasciare fare la Madonna,"[1] but it ended
by the mother giving me a free hand, with the
words, "Sia fatto la volontà di Dio e di San Gennaro Benedetto!"[2] When I made the incision and
exposed the vein, they all screamed aloud at the
sight of the blood, and when at the same moment,

[1] "Let the Blessed Virgin have her own way."
[2] "May the will of God and of Blessed San Gennaro be done!"

to my horror, the child appeared to collapse, the mother cried out with a despairing voice: "Mi muore, mi muore!" [1] At the same time one of the women pointed to the image of the Madonna, and, speechless with terror, they saw how *la lampada* flickered and went out. Silence fell over the room, and they all dropped on their knees and crossed themselves repeatedly; only the old grandmother remained where she was in her dark corner, and, rocking her head to and fro, she muttered incessantly: "Ira di Dio, ira di Dio!" [2] The mother rushed towards the image, and seizing hold of it with both hands, screamed with an almost threatening voice: "Perchè ai fatto spegnere la lampada, Madonna Santa? Voresti far spegnere così la vita della piccola? E tu fai grazie? E tu sei madre del Dio? no, no, non avresti cuore, non avresti viscere di madre." [3] She poured fresh oil into the lamp, and lighted two tapers before the image, pleading: "Ora te ne ò portato due ceri benedetti—va bene così? Tu sei contenta adesso, Madonna mia?" [4]

I sat there with the inanimate child in my arms, and I felt how they were all watching my move-

[1] "She is dying! She is dying!"
[2] "The wrath of God! The wrath of God!"
[3] "Why didst thou extinguish the lamp, O Holy Virgin? Is it thus that thou wouldest extinguish the life of my little one? And thou art full of grace? And thou art the Mother of God? No, no, thou hast not the heart, not the bowels of a mother!"
[4] "Now I have brought thee two votive candles—is all well now? Art thou satisfied now, Madonna mine?"

ments with savage and suspicious eyes. They had interpreted the extinction of the sacred lamp as a death-warrant, and nobody attempted to help me any longer.

I shall not forget that night.

With alternate prayers to the Madonna, and threats to myself, the hours wore on. I sat there staring at the child, wiping the cold perspiration now off her forehead and now off my own. I had done everything that lay in my power, and had given up all hope. I expected the child to die every moment, and I began to ask myself whether it were not my own life that I was watching over.

A cold grey dawn at last slowly entered the room, and had not my ear still detected the faint beating of the heart, I should have thought it shed its light over a corpse.

Towards morning a sort of reaction seemed to set in, the heart grew stronger, and the pulse became perceptible. She began to moan, and you should have seen the mother's face when the child at last could utter the words, "Mamma, mamma!" I had once again been mistaken, thank God!—the child was coming back to life.

I left the house soon afterwards, accompanied by the father, and after passing through a labyrinth of slums and alleys we once again stood on the Piazza Mercato. I repeated my instructions for the day, and he looked at me with a friendly glance which more than compensated me for a sleepless night.

According to our agreement we met again that same evening, and to my intense satisfaction his first words were: "Sta meglior, sia benedetto San Gennaro!" [1]

Yes, she was better, and after my visit the following evening I dared to hope that she would live. I visited her three consecutive evenings, always accompanied there and back by the father, who met me at the Piazza Mercato. I no longer insisted on going there alone, and by daylight, for I already then understood quite well why they preferred I should come after dark. The last evening I was there we had all become tremendous friends, except the old lady, who sat muttering at me the whole time, "Ammazzacane," [2] and when I went away late at night, the mother stood at the door watching me going down the slum, and long did her last words ring in my ears, "Possiate avere la pace che desirate!" [3]

When I said good-bye to the father I asked him what his name was, and he answered me "Salvatore Trapanese"—it was no business of mine as a doctor, but it was not the family initials which were en-

---

[1] "She is better, blessed be St. Gennaro!"
[2] Literally, "dog's murderer," a favourite word of cursing amongst the Neapolitan people, alas! freely used as an epithet to us doctors, but one which I especially resented.
[3] "May the peace which you desire be granted to you!"

graved upon the silver cup into which I had poured the child's medicine. Don Salvatore added that if I ever needed him, his life and his *coltello* (knife) were at my disposal. He pointed towards the corner of the Via Lavinaio, where a dirty old *ciabattino* (cobbler) sat mending a pair of boots, and told me that I had only to go to him if I wanted anything. I thanked Don Salvatore for his kindness, and he in his ignorance thanked me for the life of his child, and so we parted.

*   *   *   *   *   *

This is not much of a story, neither is it, for the matter of that, the one I meant to tell you at the outset. I often visited that part of the town, but I never came across Don Salvatore, and I soon forgot the whole affair.

It was very unsafe in the poor quarters in those days; nearly every day the newspapers gave more or less gruesome accounts of robberies and murders at night, and the Camorra seemed to display an amount of vitality which recalled the good old days when half Naples was governed by this extraordinary institution. Nothing had ever happened to me personally, and I began to wonder whether a good many of these stories were not mere moonshine.

One evening, however, whilst passing through the Vicaria quarter, I fancied I was being followed by a very suspicious-looking individual. I had some business up there, and, after having had the fellow at my heels for a long while, I certainly felt more comfortable when at last I reached the Fondaco, where I had plenty of friends. I found that the patient whom I was about to visit was already dead, and I therefore only remained in the place a short time. When I left it was quite dark, and I had not been walking for many minutes before I heard stealthy footsteps behind me. The thing to be done in these cases is to try to keep one's back free. I therefore stopped several times to allow the night wanderer to pass me; but each time the sound of his footsteps also ceased, and were it not that I now and then detected a dark shadow on the wall, I should have believed that it was nothing but the echo of my own footsteps that I heard. But Tappio growled uneasily the whole time, and as I crossed the Piazzetta dei SS. Apostoli I discovered that it was the same man who had dogged my footsteps the whole evening. Shortly afterwards I came out into the Via del Duomo, where there is considerable traffic through the night; I stopped ever so long at the corner to see whether he would follow me up, but the rascal dared not show himself in the well-lit street. The next evening I again caught sight of the same individual following me at a distance. I walked the whole way home, and as I happened to look out from my window I saw him hanging about the street corner opposite—but he missed his prey again, for I remained at home the rest of the evening.

That the fellow had some sort of design upon me I could no longer doubt, for wherever I was he suddenly turned up somewhere near, and it was evident that he tried in every way to conceal that he was shadowing me. I even found him outside the cholera cemetery one night I had been there—the burials took place at midnight, and it was early morning before I left. For the matter of that, I never saw him until after dark—like the beasts of prey he lay hidden during the day.

One gets accustomed to everything, and I very probably should have become quite used to having this man at my heels, however uncanny his appearance, but for the fact that my suspicions ere long became confirmed in the most unexpected manner.

I stood one evening on the Molo (harbour) watching the twilight fall over the gulf, whilst high up against the darkening firmament old Vesuvius lit the lamps in his gigantic lighthouse. Suddenly I saw my man coming running along the pier, jump into a boat, and in a desperate hurry row out of the harbour. Immediately afterwards two carabineers jumped into another boat and gave chase to him. In less than a minute at least a hundred people had assembled on the shore watching the chase in the greatest excitement, and I heard from a promising urchin beside me, who was shouting "Coraggio! coraggio!" to the fugitive, that the man they were trying to catch was a well-known Camorrist. Lots of small boats were just coming in from the day's fishing, and it was easy to see that they did their best to get in the way of the carabineers' boat. One of the carabineers pointed his revolver at the fugitive, but scarcely had he time to fire before the Camorrist threw himself into the sea. It had now become so dark that I was unable to distinguish anything, but the others assured me that he was unhurt, and could be seen swimming towards a large boat which was just hoisting sail to go out fishing for the night; she bore away towards the swimmer, and it seemed as if he would succeed in reaching her. Once in the boat he would be in safety, and, protected by the darkness, he could easily land somewhere on the coast—I have sailed with smugglers myself, and know that coast-guards do not suffer from insomnia. The people around me made no secret of their sympathy for the Camorrist, and I am bound to say that I found myself hoping that he would succeed in getting away—I am afraid this sounds very bad, but I seldom side with the police in this part of the world.

Official justice, however, gained the day this time; they overtook him, and soon afterwards landed with their prisoner. He was handcuffed, and he was so exhausted by his long struggle that he could hardly drag himself along between his two captors. The crowd accompanied him down the much-dreaded road to the prison of San Francesco. But I remained riveted to the spot, for as he passed me the prisoner raised his head, and his eyes met mine with an extraordinary expression of reproach.

The next day I read in the *Pungolo* that a dangerous Camorrist had been arrested on the Molo after a desperate struggle, and that the police at last believed they were on the track of a gang of Camorrists who were guilty of all sorts of crimes.

I had succeeded in getting quite a large practice in the poor quarter, and I spent most of my time there. Experience had taught me how to deal with these people, and I had secured several good friends among them. It seemed to me that of late the circle of my acquaintances had considerably increased; wherever I went some ragged fellows were always nodding at me, and when returning home at night I was constantly greeted with a friendly "Buona sera, Eccellenza!" by unknown night-wanderers. The cabmen in the Piazza Mercato began to crack their whips as soon as they caught sight of me, calling out with an intonation of the voice which was not the usual one: "Signŏ, vulit' a mme!" [1] and even if I did not care to drive, they were nevertheless just as friendly. If I entered a little *osteria*, I often noticed that after a sign exchanged between some

[1] "Do you want me?"

of the guests and the landlord, the latter redoubled his attentions to me, and it even happened that having served me with a bottle of wine, he came and replaced it with first-rate *vino vecchio*, after a colloquy of lively gesticulations between himself and my cabman, who sat on his box outside waiting for me.

I was, of course, flattered by all this, but I could not help beginning to wonder at the unexpected extension of my circle of acquaintances. But what puzzled me most was that for some time I had noticed that another fellow had begun to follow me wherever I went. His appearance was, to say the least of it, as doubtful as that of his predecessor, and it was soon evident that he had adopted the other man's inexplicable system of shadowing me.

One day I was driving down towards Porta Capuana with a cabby who, notwithstanding that I had no recollection of having met him before, was overwhelming in his attentions to me. We drove past the prison of San Francesco, and just as we passed the gate my driver winked mysteriously at me, and this is the conversation that took place—I think I had better translate our Neapolitan vernacular, or else you would never understand it.

"Has Eccellenza been to see him?" asked the cabman.

"Whom?"

"Does not Eccellenza know that he was arrested,

and is imprisoned here? But it was his own fault; he had no business to follow Eccellenza down on the Molo, where Eccellenza was in no need of protection and where, besides, he was sure to come across lots of policemen, and it is not at all Eccellenza's fault."

"But sapristi, whom are you talking about?"

"Il fratello del vostro amico," [1] said the driver, with another wink of his eye.

It was the brother of Don Salvatore Trapanese who had been arrested on the Molo.

.   .   .   .   .   .

My wanderings came to an unexpected end the very next day, for I fell ill myself. It was not much to speak of, but it came upon me very suddenly indeed. I must have fainted straight off in the street, for when I opened my eyes and looked around, I found myself half-lying in a cab, and opposite me sat a policeman, pale as death, staring at me with an expression of absolute terror in his face. I tried to recollect what had happened, and for what sort of crime I had been taken in charge; but my head was altogether out of gear, and as for the Camorra, Don Salvatore, myself, and the San Francesco prison, I had muddled them all up together.

"Sta un poco meglio?" [2] said the policeman.

[1] "The brother of your friend."
[2] "Do you feel better?"

"Gnorsì," [1] answered I.

"Coraggio, un altro poco siamo arrivati!" [2] were his next words.

We drove along the Strada Piliero, and the wind from the sea blew over my forehead. My thoughts began to clear up, and I suddenly remembered that I was a doctor. I asked the policeman to give me a bottle of ether I had in my pocket, and he put his fingers in my coat pocket as cautiously as if he had put them in a furnace. Here and there the people in the street turned round to look at us, and I saw them make the sign of the cross as we drove past.

We were on our way to the cholera hospital.

My brain began to work quite well, and it seemed to me that the cholera hospital was a very uncanny sort of place to go to. I discovered that the policeman was entirely of my opinion. At my request we pulled up before a little *osteria*, where I drank the policeman's health in a stiff glass of brandy which felt like dynamite, whilst he and the cabman had a litre of wine between them. I assured the policeman that I was in no need of a doctor, that I was a doctor myself, in fact, and that certainly I was not down with cholera; and the good-natured fellow told me that he had been sure of that all along—"un poco di febbre," [3] that was all.

I got home all right, but remember nothing after

[1] "Yes."
[2] "Courage! another moment and we shall be there."
[3] "A little fever."

entering the house. Soon afterwards I found that Cæsare was putting a bit of ice in my mouth, and as I opened my eyes I saw that the evening sun was still shining in the room. But Cæsare said that it was not the same sun; I had been lying in my bed for twenty-four hours, said he—I had skipped over the whole of that time in my memory, and I may just as well do the same here. I asked Cæsare— Cæsare was my valet, butler, cook, anything you like—if I had cholera, and I quite fancied that it was somebody else who was speaking, for I did not recognise my own voice; it sounded cracked, like that of an old woman. Cæsare answered that he was not quite sure, but he feared it was so—his opinion was not without weight, for together we had seen his wife and two children die of it.

Yes, it was of course possible that it was cholera, although the symptoms did not seem to me quite typical; but cholera was always in one's thoughts in those days.

And I felt curious to see what the night would bring forth.

Cæsare had gone out to get more ice, he said, and I lay there all by myself. When the head is weary one can only think sad thoughts, and at last one tries not to think at all. One feels so tired, and one only longs to be in peace and have done with it. To die is not so terrible after all, but cowardly natures fear prolonged suffering. It is a psychological

error to believe that to witness the agony of others
makes us more familiar with sombre death; this is
only true as long as it is a question of seeing others
die. But when, after having well thought it over,
one comes to the conclusion that maybe the moment
is at hand when one's own life is to end, then one
wishes that one had never seen what it is to die.
"Be a man," one says to oneself, "and if you did not
know how to live, at least show that you know how
to die!" Still the imagination ceaselessly conjures
up visions of those anguished eyes that so often met
one's own in search for hope, when, as a doctor, one
stood beside a deathbed; those stiffening fingers
which spasmodically clutched at the bed-clothes,
even as a drowning man will catch at a straw, and
gropingly tried to get hold of one's hand to cling
to life; those panting breasts which strained every
muscle to get a little more air in order to prolong
the desperate struggle with the executioner who
slowly but surely was strangling his victim. Yes,
Heine was right: "Der Tod ist nichts, aber das
Sterben ist eine schändliche Erfindung." [1]

The window stood wide open, and from where I
lay I could see out over the gulf. It looked so happy
and bright out there, and it seemed to me as if the
shores had decked themselves in all their beauty to
bid me farewell. I looked across to Capri, which lay
there in rosy slumber, and I thought it so hard

[1] "Death is nothing, but dying is an ignominious invention."

should I now have to depart from the land I loved so well. A light mist flew over the gulf, and I heard friendly voices from my youth calling me by name.

So all became silent, twilight fell around me, and I felt so lonely.

I stretched out my hand for my friend, but he was not there; I called him by name, but he did not come. I tried to think he had gone out with Cæsare, and breathlessly I listened for the sound of his steps on the stairs. The door was quietly opened, and Cæsare entered on tiptoe.

"Where is he?" I asked; Cæsare tried to reassure me, saying he would come back directly; but I forced him to tell me the truth, and then I understood that I was lonely indeed.

Cæsare had been standing at the window, had seen me return, and had carried me upstairs, for I had fainted as I got out of the cab. The driver had seen nothing of my dog, and Cæsare had been so frightened at my appearance that, sorry as I am to have to say it, he had made no inquiries about him till a few minutes ago, when he had gone down to send for the consul; and I am not even sure that it was for Tappio's sake that he had done so. I tried to be angry with Cæsare, but I was so tired that I did not succeed.

The consul came shortly afterwards. He was a very nice fellow, but he had completely misunderstood the situation, and seemed to believe that some-

thing else was the matter. However, after he had
heard of my loss, he promised me to do all that lay
in his power to find my dog. He added that he
hoped to be more successful in finding the dog than
he had been in his efforts to find me. He had heaps
of letters and telegrams for me, he said, and a few
days ago he had received a telegram directing him
to find out whether I were "dead or alive": he had
tried his best to discover me, but all his inquiries
had been absolutely futile.

I laughed in my sleeve, sad as I felt, and sug-
gested that it might be as well to wait a day or two
before answering that telegram. Cæsare accompanied him downstairs, and I heard how my facto-
tum whispered to the consul: "Parla con lo cane
come era un Cristiano." [1]

Later in the evening I got a line from the consul
to say that every policeman in Naples had received
orders to be on the lookout for the dog, and that I
had every reason to hope for the best.

My illness did not come to much, after all, and
the whole night I lay awake waiting for one of the
well-known symptoms which was wanting to de-
clare itself. I felt rather better the next day, but
was far too worried to bother much about myself,
as you may well imagine.

But perhaps you are laughing at me as you read
this, and, if so, you are welcome to laugh as much

[1] "He speaks to the dog as though he were a human being."

as you like. But I can tell you that I did not laugh as I lay there thinking of the faithful friend I had lost, the friend who had shared joys and sorrows with me for ten whole years. Had he perhaps fallen into brutal hands who ill-treated him? Did he perhaps sit chained, anxiously waiting that I should come and deliver him?—I who could not even stand on my feet!

I had taken into my head that were I only able to get out I should find him at once, and I nearly cried over my impotence. I prayed and threatened Cæsare to make him help me into my clothes and carry me down into a cab, but he turned a deaf ear to all my entreaties. That same afternoon the consul came to see me; he had no news of my dog, and I was now sure that he was lost to me for ever. The consul tried to console me, and told me that one of his colleagues had lost his dog twice and got it back, and that he now paid to a Camorrist five lire a year as a guarantee that his dog should not be stolen from him any more.

After the consul had left, Cæsare and I held a council of war. Our confidence in the official authorities had never been very great, and Cæsare cherished an antipathy towards the police which surpassed my own. The same evening Cæsare went down to the Piazza Mercato to try and find the old *ciabattino*. About eleven o'clock that night I received a visit from an individual whose appearance

in my room at night under any other circumstances
would have frightened me to death. He greeted me
with great familiarity, and asked me if I recognised
him, but I was obliged to confess that I did not—
he looked like the devil himself. He brought a greeting from Don Salvatore, who was unavoidably pre-
vented from coming, but he begged to assure me
that he himself was my very good friend. I thanked
him for his kind feelings towards me, and told him
all about Tappio. I emptied the contents of my
purse on to the bed, and I told him that all I possessed should be given to whoever brought the dog
back—I am always short of funds, but I believe
there might have been about two hundred lire. He
listened attentively, and I shall never forget his
words when I finished speaking: "Se non è morto
sara çça domani sera!" [1] I feared that he was much
too confident, and I told him I knew well what cunning rascals those dog-stealers were. But when he
answered me with great dignity, "Sono tutti miei
amici," [2] I felt that I had underrated his importance. I thanked him for the hope his visit had
brought me, and he wished me good-bye. He turned
round in the doorway and invoked the protection of
the Blessed Virgin and San Gennaro on my behalf.
And that very moment I suddenly recognised him.
He was the man I had so often seen following my

[1] "You shall have him back to-morrow evening if he be not dead."
[2] "They are all friends of mine."

steps after Salvatore's brother had been arrested on the Molo!

I slept better that night, and next morning it was evident that the consul might telegraph home that I was "alive" without any fear of being put to an extra expense by having to contradict the news. But as the hours dragged on I grew more and more restless. Amongst other things I remembered as I lay there that I had been rather hard, not to say unjust, to poor Tappio for a mere trifle the very evening before I was taken ill, and you cannot imagine how this thought continually came back to my mind, and how it tortured me.

Evening came, and yet no news. Cæsare had received orders to stand and watch down in the street, and since he had now begun to obey me again, he really had gone and left me for awhile. I was so tired with all the anxiety, that at last I fell into a sort of half-slumber. I do not know how long I lay there in the dark, but I know how I was awakened. Cæsare rushed into the room, I heard a panting on the stairs which made me try to jump out of bed, and Tappio dashed in, dragging Don Salvatore after him. Don Salvatore let go the rope, and my dear old dog came bounding up to the bed. He put his forepaws on my shoulders, and laid his great head softly on my breast. His glossy coat was ragged and bloody, and a thick rope was tied round his neck. Neither of us said a word, but we have

never been in need of words to understand each
other. He crept nearer and nearer to me, and at last
he crawled on to the bed, big as he was; and you
may be sure that that day he was allowed to do so.

Don Salvatore remained standing at the door.
He looked pale and haggard, but notwithstanding
that his coat was all in rags, one could still discern
the white borders which were stitched upon it.[1] I
held out my hand, and thanked him for the joy he
had brought me. He looked quite shy, and I noticed
that he avoided my eye: "Sono uomo di mala vita,"
said he; "e non sono degno di toccar la vostra
mano." [2]

I certainly had no reason for being severe on any
one, but I had several reasons for not being so, as
I told him.

I then gave him the money, but he put it back
on the bed with these words: "Voi avete salvato la
figliuola, io ho trovato, lo cane—va bene così!" [3]

He threw his ragged cloak over his shoulder and
went away.

But I believe that I owe Don Salvatore more
than my dog.

[1] When a child falls ill the parents make a vow to the Blessed Virgin
for its recovery. They promise to wear her colours for a certain
period, sometimes for years, and nothing in the world would induce
them to lay them aside before the expiration of the time. Brown, with
a binding of white, is what is worn in honour of the Madonna del
Carmine, white with red bindings for the Madonna delle Salette,
etc., etc.

[2] "I am a bad man, and not worthy of touching your hand."

[3] "You saved the little girl, I found the dog—that's all right!"

CHAPTER XIV

LA MADONNA DEL BUON CAMMINO

La Madonna del Buon Cammino

THE doctor had often noticed him standing in the doorway of his little chapel eagerly scanning the dirty lane, and, already at a distance, friendly salutations were exchanged between them in the usual Neapolitan fashion of waving hands, with "Buon giorno, Don Dionisio!" "Ben venuto, Signor Dottore!"

Often, too, he had looked in at the old deserted cloister garden, with its dried-up fountain and a few pale autumn roses against the wall of the little sanctuary. Don Dionisio had often told him of the many miracles of the Madonna of Buon Cammino. The Madonna of Buon Cammino stood there quite alone in her half-ruined shrine, where a solitary little oil-lamp struggled with the darkness within. With great solemnity Don Dionisio had drawn aside the curtain which veiled his Madonna from profane eyes; and tenderly as a mother he had arranged the tattered fringes of her robe, which threatened to fall to pieces altogether. And the doctor had gazed with compassionate wonder at the pale waxen image with the unconscious smile on the impassive features, which in Don Dionisio's eyes represented the highest physical and spiritual beauty. "Come è bella, come è simpatica!" [1] said he, looking up at his Madonna.

Inside the old church of Santa Maria del Carmine, close by, hundreds of votive candles were burning before the altars, and night and day the people flocked there to implore the mighty Madonna's protection. Mothers took the ring from their finger to hang it as a sacred offering round the Madonna's neck, girls drew the strings of coral out of their dark plaits to adorn the rich robe of the statue, and, with brows pressed against the worn marble floor, strong men knelt, murmuring prayers for help and mercy.

Death dwelt in the slums of Naples. Three times the miraculous image of the Madonna del Carmine had been carried round the piazza in solemn procession to protect the people of the Mercato from the dreaded plague, and many miracles were reported of dying people brought back to life having kissed the hem of her garment.

The doctor had seen Don Dionisio vanish into his little portico with a disdainful shrug when the procession of Santa Maria del Carmine passed by, and he had more than once caught the old priest in the act of incredulously shaking his head at the

[1] "How beautiful, how sympathetic she is!"

wondrous tales of some of the far-famed Madonna's miracles repeated to him by one gossip or another, he had succeeded in detaining on her way to the famous shrine.

"What, after all, has your Madonna done for you, you people of Mercato?" he would cry out mockingly. "If she is as powerful as that, why has she not saved Naples from the cholera? And here, in the midst of her own quarter, in Mercato, whose inhabitants for centuries have knelt before her, what has she done to prevent the disease spreading here? Do not people die every day round her own sanctuary, round the very Piazza del Mercato, in spite of all your prayers, in spite of all your votive candles? 'Altro che la Madonna del Carmine!'[1]

"What about our side of the piazza where there is no cholera, and where none will ever come, I should like to know who you have to thank for that, if not the holy Madonna del Buon Cammino, who stretches her protecting hand over you although you do not deserve it, although you leave her sanctuary dark and take all your offerings to the other Madonnas, whatever their names may be! And yet you cannot see in your blindness that the blessed Madonna del Buon Cammino is far more powerful than all your Madonnas put together! 'Altro che la Madonna del Carmine!' "

But no one seemed to take any heed of the old

[1] "Madonna del Carmine indeed!"

man's expostulations, no votive candles dispersed
the darkness within the chapel of the blessed Madonna del Buon Cammino, and no lips murmured
her name in their prayers for help and protection
against the dreaded scourge. Had they not Santa
Maria del Carmine close by, who from all time had
been the patron saint of the quarter, who had helped
them through so much distress, and consoled them
in so much misery? Was there not in her church
that miraculous Christ out of whose pierced side
blood trickled every Good Friday, and whose hair
the priests solemnly cut every Christmas? And if
the Madonna del Carmine was not enough for
them, had they not the venerable Madonna del
Colera, who saved their city in the year 1834 from
the same sickness which now raged amongst them?
And in the Harbour quarter close by, did not the
Madonna del Porto Salvo stand in her sumptuous
chapel dressed in silk and gold brocade, ready to
listen to their prayers? Was there not by the Banchi
Nuovi the far-famed Madonna dell' Aiuto, who
would certainly not belie her name of Helper in
the hour of need? Had they not La Madonna dell'
Addolorata with the mantle of solid silver and the
black velvet robe, whose folds no one had ever kissed
without gaining comfort and peace? Had they not
La Madonna dell' Immacolata, whose sky-blue garment was strewn with gold stars from the vault of
heaven itself? Had they not La Madonna di Salette

in her purple skirt dyed with the blood of martyrs?
And did not San Gennaro himself stand in his shining dome above—he, the patron saint of Naples,
whose congealed blood flows anew every year, he
who protected the city of his predilection from
plague and famine, and commanded the flowing
lava of Vesuvius to stop short before its very gates?
But La Madonna del Buon Cammino—who had
ever heard of her? Who knew whence she came or
who had witnessed with their own eyes a single
miracle worked by her hand? What kind of Madonna was that whose shrine remained without candles or flowers, and whose mantle was in rags?
"Non tiene neppure capelli, la vostra Madonna!" [1]
an old woman had once shouted in Don Dionisio's
face, to the great delight of the passers-by. The
effect of this argument had been crushing, and Don
Dionisio had disappeared in great fury inside his
portico, and had not been seen again for several
days.

The doctor's way lay in that direction one evening, and he determined to visit his old friend. From
inside the chapel he heard Don Dionisio with mighty
voice intoning an old Latin hymn in honour of his
Madonna.

"Consolatrix miserorum,
Suscitatrix mortuorum,
Mortis rumpe retia;

[1] "Your Madonna has not even got any hair on her head!"

Intendentes tuae laudi,
Nos attende, nos exaudi,
Nos a morte libera!"

He lifted the curtain before the door, and in the light of the little oil-lamp he saw Don Dionisio on his knees before the image of his Madonna, very busy brushing the cobwebs off an enormous old wig of an indescribable colour. His anger had not yet subsided. "Dicono che non tiene capelli!" he called out as soon as he caught sight of the doctor; "mo vogliamo vedere chi tieni i più belli capelli!" [1] And with a triumphant glance at his visitor he placed the wig upon the bald head of La Madonna del Buon Cammino. "Come è bella, come è simpatica!" said he, with sparkling eyes, while he arranged as well as he could the entangled curls round the forehead of the image.

When the doctor went away Don Dionisio's wrath had subsided, and again he took up his position in the little portico in excellent spirits, quite ready to fight both on the offensive and defensive for his Madonna's sake. That same evening the doctor was told that there had been a case of cholera in a *fondaco* close by the street in which Don Dionisio lived, and he went to inquire about it early the next morning. As he passed the chapel he caught sight of the old fellow already at his post,

---

[1] "They say she has got no hair; but we shall soon see who has the most beautiful hair!"

rubbing his hands and looking very cheerful, and the doctor had not the heart to tell him that it began to look as if even the protection of his Madonna would now fail them. But Don Dionisio waved his hand eagerly as soon as he caught sight of the doctor, and when he was still some distance off he called out, so as to be heard throughout the whole lane, "Ecco il colera!" See now what I have always said! Here you have got it because you would not believe in La Madonna del Buon Cammino; now you are all of you going to see what becomes of those who believe more in the Madonna del Carmine than in her! "Ecco il colera!" in our very midst, "Ecco il colera!"

The lane was full of people, who terror-struck had fled out of their houses to pray in the churches and before the shrines at the street corners, and some of them stopped irresolutely in front of the chapel to listen to Don Dionisio's threatening prophecy of death to every one who had dared to brave the anger of the blessed Madonna del Buon Cammino. The *fondaco* seemed quite empty, for as many as were able had run away at the first alarm; but, guided by the sound of praying voices, the doctor came at last to a dark hole, where the usual sight met his eyes. Round the door some kneeling *commare* [1] in earnest prayer; stretched out at full length upon the floor a mother wringing her hands

[1] Gossips.

in despair; and in a corner the livid face of a child,
half-hidden under a heap of ragged coverings. The
little girl was quite cold, her eyelids half shut, and
her pulse scarcely perceptible. Now and again a
convulsive trembling passed over her; but except
for that she lay there quite motionless and insensible
—cholera! At the head of the bed lay a picture of
the Madonna del Carmine, and the doctor gathered
from the muttering of the women, that the wonder-
working Madonna had been brought there the evening before. Now and then the mother lifted her
head and looked searchingly at the doctor, and it
seemed to him as if he could read something like
confidence in her anguished eyes. And yet it appeared as if he could do nothing. Ether injections,
frictions, all the usual remedies proved fruitless to
bring the warmth of life back, and the pulse grew
weaker and weaker. Again the doctor noticed to
his surprise the same trusting expression in the
mother's eyes when she looked at him, and he determined to put his new remedy to the test. He
knew well there was nothing to lose, for left to herself the child was evidently dying; but for some
time he had been haunted by an idea that maybe
there was still everything to gain in a case like
this. Nobody paid any further attention to what he
did; the mother lay with her forehead pressed
against the floor, imploring the Madonna to take
her own life in exchange for the child's; and

amongst the *commare* the prayers had ceased, and in their place a lively discussion had broken out as to whether it would not be better to fetch some other Madonna, since the Madonna del Carmine would not help them in spite of all their prayers, in spite of the candles before her shrine, in spite of the mother's promise to dress the child in the Madonna's colour for a whole year, if only its life could be spared. The child was quite insensible, and the doctor set to work without further delay. When all was finished he slightly touched the mother's shoulder, and whilst she stared at him, as if she hardly understood his words, he said that there was no time to lose if they wished to try the good offices of another Madonna, and why not the Madonna del Buon Cammino, whose chapel was close by? There was a deep silence, and it was plain that his suggestion did not meet with the slightest sympathy. He, however, pretended to take their silence for consent, and with a little difficulty succeeded in persuading one of the women, whom he knew well, to go in search of the Madonna del Buon Cammino.

Don Dionisio came like a shot with his Madonna in his arms. He placed the little oil-lamp at the feet of the image, and eagerly began to intone the hymn to his Madonna with an occasional furious side-glance at the image of her powerful rival, before which the mother still lay prostrated. In the

doorway the *commare* were muttering all sorts of
opprobrious remarks about his idol: "Vatene farti
un altra gonnella, poverella! Benedetto San Gennaro, che brutta faccia che l'hanno dato, povera
vecchia!" [1]

Suddenly they became silent, and in breathless
amazement they all stared at the pale waxen assistant of the doctor in his fight for the child's life.
For from the closely compressed lips of the dying
girl a subdued moan was heard, and the half-
opened eyes turned slowly towards the Madonna
del Buon Cammino. All crossed themselves repeatedly; and the doctor felt the child's pulse grow
stronger, and the warmth of life slowly begin to
spread over the icy limbs. The terror of death
stared from her now wide-open eyes, and she cried
with half-broken voice: "Salvatemi! Salvatemi!
Madonna Sanctissima!" [2] In a still more powerful
voice Don Dionisio proceeded with his chant, and
all those in the room were now murmuring the
name of the blessed Madonna del Buon Cammino.
Soon afterwards Don Dionisio left the *fondaco* in
triumph, closely followed by almost all its inhabitants. The child was then quite conscious; and nobody doubted that the holy Madonna del Buon
Cammino had worked a miracle.

The doctor remained for a while at the child's

[1] "Go and make thyself another gown, poor thing! Blessed San
Gennaro, what an ugly face they have given her, poor old creature!"
[2] "Save me, save me, most holy Madonna!"

side, watching with the keenest interest its slow but sure return to consciousness. Late at night, when he looked in again, the improvement was so marked that it was probable the child would live. In the *fondaco* and surrounding slums, nothing was talked of but the new miracle; and on his way home for the first time the doctor saw light streaming from the chapel of the Madonna del Buon Cammino.

He did not sleep a wink that night, for he could not keep his thoughts away from what he had witnessed in the morning, and he could hardly restrain his impatience to meet with a fresh case on which to repeat the experiment.

He had not to wait long. The same night another woman in the *fondaco* was attacked, and when he saw her the next day, she was already so bad, that it seemed as if she might die at any moment. His advice to fetch the Madonna del Buon Cammino was now taken without hesitation, and whilst everybody's attention was fixed upon Don Dionisio and his image, the doctor could busy himself with his patient, undisturbed by any suspicious and interfering eyes.

Here again a speedy and decided reaction set in, which became more and more pronounced during the day; and that same evening the rumour spread through the alleys of the Mercato of a second miracle by the wonder-working Madonna del Buon Cammino.

Thus began those strange never-to-be-forgotten days, when, insensible to fatigue, yea! to hunger, the doctor went day and night from bed to bed, borne on the strong wings of an idea which almost blinded his sight, and made all his scepticism waver. He would come with Don Dionisio at his heels to meet the usual sight of some poor half-dead creature for whom it would seem that human skill could do nothing, and when, an hour or two later, the Madonna del Buon Cammino was carried away in solemn procession, followed by the deepest devotion of the crowd, he would slip out unnoticed, forgetful of everything, in silent wonder at the sudden and constant improvement which his remedy had effected, an improvement which often seemed like a resurrection.

Ah! he had gone down there to Naples where it seemed as if he had done a lot to help others, but where in reality he had done much more to help himself—where he had almost forgotten his own misery. His experience of cholera was already a large one, he knew about as much as others knew. He knew that fate reigns over death as over life. Method after method he had tried honestly and conscientiously, and he had learnt that in spite of Professor Koch, in spite of the discovery of the microbes, his helplessness was as great as ever when it came to the treatment of a cholera patient. So he had wandered round the streets of Naples with remedies in his hands in which he had little faith himself, and words of encouragement on his lips, but hopeless scepticism in his heart.

And now this last experiment, so bold that he had almost shrunk from trying it, which had resulted in an unbroken series of successes in the midst of an epidemic with an enormous mortality! Once again he was a doctor and nothing more. With redoubled zeal he watched every new case, scarcely for a minute did he leave his patient's side, and with increasing excitement he observed every symptom with his former scepticism—and yet the fact remained, for a whole week not a single fatal case!

He had almost forgotten that Don Dionisio and the Madonna del Buon Cammino followed in his wake wherever he went—he had forgotten them as he had forgotten himself. Now and then his eyes would fall upon his unconscious assistants, and he was the last to grudge the old man and his Madonna the lion's share in his success, which the onlookers unhesitatingly bestowed upon them. Don Dionisio seemed to need no more rest than the doctor, he was on his legs day and night with his Madonna. His face shone with ecstasy, and he enjoyed to the full his short triumph. The Madonna del Buon Cammino was now clothed in a flame-coloured silken mantle, a diadem of huge glass beads encircled her brow, and strung together around her neck hung numbers of rings and gold

ear-rings. Night and day votive candles were
lighted in her chapel, and on the walls once so bare
now hung "ex votos" of all possible kinds, thank-
offerings for deliverance from sickness and death.
The chapel was always full of people, kneeling fer-
vently before that mighty Madonna who had performed so many miracles, and who shielded the
slums around her sanctuary from the dreaded
scourge. For, to his amazement, the doctor had
heard Don Dionisio prophesy that as long as the
lights burned in the chapel of the Madonna del
Buon Cammino, the cholera would never dare to
invade her street.

It was now that terror fell upon the poor of
Naples, that the infection, swift as fire, burst forth
over all the alleys and slums of the poor quarters.
It was now that people fell down in the street as
though struck by lightning; that the dying and
dead lay side by side in almost every house; that
the very omnibuses of the street had to be utilised
to carry the dead to the Campo Santo dei Colerosi,[1]
where over a thousand corpses every night filled
the enormous grave. It was now that trembling
hands broke down the walls with which modern
times had hidden the old shrines at the street corners, that the people in wild fury stormed the
Duomo to force the priests to carry San Gennaro
himself down to their slums. It was now that

[1] Cholera cemetery.

anxiety reached the borders of frenzy, that despair
began to howl like rage, that from trembling lips
prayers and curses fell in alternating confusion,
that knives gleamed in hands which just before had
convulsively grasped rosary and crucifix.

The doctor and his friend went their way as before, unmoved by the increasing horrors which surrounded them. And wherever they went Death gave
way before them. The doctor needed all his self-
control to persist in his scepticism of old, and before his eyes he saw as in a mirage the goal of his
most daring dreams. As for Don Dionisio, whose
freedom of thought had been benumbed so long,
no questioning doubt ever disturbed his serenity, and
the doctor had recognised the futility of any attempt to endeavour to restrain the old fellow in his
buoyant certitude of victory.

The epidemic had now reached its climax, almost
every house in the quarter was infected and still
Don Dionisio's prophecy held good, for not a single
case had occurred in the street of the Madonna del
Buon Cammino.

The doctor had been told by an old crone, that a
woman was dying in one of the *bassi* in Orto del
Conte, and that her husband had been *avvelenato*[1]
in the hospital the day before. He went there the
same evening, but it was with great difficulty that
he succeeded in making his way through the hostile

[1] Poisoned.

crowd which had assembled in front of the infected
house. He heard that the husband had been removed almost by force to the hospital, that he had
there died, and that when, a couple of hours later,
an ambulance had come to take his wife, who had
been seized in her turn, the crowd had opposed it
fiercely, a *carabiniere* had been stabbed, and the
others had had to save their lives by flight. As usual
the unfortunate doctors had to bear the blame, and
he heard all around him the well-known epithets of
assassino! [1] *avvelenatore!* [2] All his attempts to make
friends with them and gain their confidence having
failed completely, there was nothing to do but to
await Don Dionisio's arrival. As soon as he came
everybody's attention was at once centred in him
and his Madonna, and they all fell on their knees in
fervent prayer without taking the slightest notice
either of the patient or the doctor. The woman was
in *Stadium algidum,* [3] but her pulse was still perceptible. Strong in the confidence of his previous
successes, the doctor went to work. He had hardly
finished before the heart began to flag. Just as Don
Dionisio with triumphant voice announced that the
miracle was accomplished, the death agony set in,
and it was with the greatest difficulty that the doctor succeeded in keeping up the action of the heart
until Don Dionisio and his Madonna had been

[1] "Assassin!"   [2] "Poisoner!"
[3] The state of collapse, characteristic of cholera, when the body
becomes cold.

safely got out of the house, followed by the crowd
outside in solemn procession. A few minutes later
the doctor slipped away like a thief, and ran for his
life to the corner of the Via del Duomo, where he
knew he would be in safety.

The same night three of his patients died. He
did his utmost to prevent Don Dionisio accompanying him the following day, but in vain. Every one
of the sick he visited and treated that day died before his eyes.

The wings which had borne him during those
wondrous days had fallen from him, and dead tired
he wandered home in the evening with Don Dionisio
at his side. They bade each other good-night in
front of the chapel of the Madonna del Buon Cammino, and in the flickering light of the lamp before
her shrine the doctor saw a deathly pallor over-
spread the face of his friend. The old man tottered
and fell, with the Madonna in his arms. The doctor carried him into the chapel and laid him upon
the straw bed where he slept, in a corner behind a
curtain. He placed the Madonna del Buon Cammino carefully on her stand, and poured oil for the
night into the little lamp which burned over her
head. Don Dionisio motioned with his hand to be
moved nearer, and the doctor dragged his bed forward to the pedestal of the image. "Come è bella,
come è simpatica!" said he, with feeble voice. He
lay there quite motionless and silent, with his eyes

intently fixed upon his beloved Madonna. The doctor sat all night long by his side, whilst he grew
weaker and weaker and slowly became cold. One
votive candle after another flickered and went out,
and the shadows fell deeper and deeper in the
chapel of the Madonna del Buon Cammino. Then
all was dark, and only the little oil-lamp of old
threw a trembling light over the pale waxen image
with the unconscious smile upon the impassive features.

The next day the doctor fainted in the street, and
was picked up and taken to the Cholera Hospital.
And, indomitable as fate, Death swept over the
street of the Madonna del Buon Cammino, over
Vicolo del Monaco. For it was Vicolo del Monaco—
that name which filled Naples with terror, and
which, through the reports of the newspapers became known to the whole world as the place where
the cholera raged its fiercest.[1]

·   ·   ·   ·   ·   ·

The dark little chapel, which had sheltered the
confused devotion of the old visionary, has been
razed to the ground by the new order of things
which has dawned over Naples at last, and Vicolo
del Monaco is no more. Don Dionisio sank unconscious from the dim thought-world of his supersti-

[1] Almost the whole alley died. An official report stated that there
were over thirty cases in a single hour.

tion into the impenetrable darkness of the great grave up there on the Campo Santo dei Colerosi.

The other, the fool, who for a moment had believed he could command Death to stop short in his triumphant march, he is still alive, but with the bitter vision of reality for all time overshadowing his sight. So will he sink, he also, into the great grave of oblivion; and of all those who lived and suffered in the Vicolo del Monaco nothing will remain—nothing.

Behind a curtain in some dark little chapel stands the Madonna del Buon Cammino, with the unconscious smile upon the impassive features.

CHAPTER XV

PORTA SAN PAOLO

Porta San Paolo

(THE PROTESTANT CEMETERY IN ROME)

"It might make one in love with death, to be buried in so sweet a place."—SHELLEY.

CAMELLIAS glisten in sombre splendour amidst the laurel and honeysuckle, the myrtle is in bloom, and fair roses twine garlands round the stems of cypress trees. Narcissi and lilies rise from the high grass, and overhead the thrush sings the summer evening's shimmering farewell to the dying day.

Fair garden, whither the wanderer wends his way, are they the poppies of oblivion that breathe among thy roses, is it the peace of dreamland that rustles through thy darkening cypresses?

But seest thou not the white crosses among the leaves and flowers, seest thou not the broken columns half hidden by the ivy? Bend asunder the branches, that have woven the resignation of years over the sorrowful lines written upon the stone, look down among the lilies and violets, and behold they flower upon graves!

The soil thou treadst upon is holy; here lives the memory of those who once were men.

From far came they hither these silent sleepers, wide around the world had their winged thoughts flown ere they gathered here into eternal rest.

Many lands had reared them, many paths led them on through life, by sunlit heights or through the shadow of the valleys, in the triumph of happiness, or bent under the burden of grief—until at last they reached their goal, the night-covered plain into which heights and valleys have merged, where the jubilant voices of victory resound no more, and where the wail of sorrow is hushed.

Side by side have they lain down here to sleep. The laurel over their head crowns alike the urn strewn by the immortelles of Fame, and the humble mound where the grass grows wild. From darkening cypresses slowly descends the night of oblivion alike upon the name which history has hewn in the marble, as upon the nameless whose doings are long forgotten. Maybe there lingers still the light of a yearning memory round the simple wooden cross long after the stately mausoleum lies wrapped in darkness, maybe among the field flowers and grasses of the mound love watches through the still night in the breath of the violets long after the fragrant roses have fallen asleep.

The inscriptions tell who they were that death brought here, and, pensive, the wanderer reads their names. He reads the year a name was given them; he reads the year it was taken from them: but what of joy and what of sorrow lies between these years he knows not.

They were artists many of those who lie beneath the crosses.

Full of enthusiasm and young joy they journeyed hither, hailing the Eternal City as their mother. And Rome took them to her arms, reared their souls with her strong thoughts, and told them among the ruins of the Flavian amphitheatre and the imperial palaces on the Palatine hill, her own proud story and the marble-shining legend of Hellas.

Here they dreamt their fairest dream. Here they were consecrated Soldiers of the Light at the altar of the eternal Ideal, here in this same Rome, where Michael Angelo raised his mighty cupola over the temple ground of antique art, and Raphael awoke the butterfly-winged Eros of beauty from the long slumber of mediæval night to the spring morning of the Renaissance.

And thus when they fancied they were nearing their goal, and they already stretched out their hands towards the flying Daphne of their ideal, then the slender limbs grew into a sombre cypress where a heart beat no more beneath the bark; and not to the jubilant Capitol of fame, but to the Silent Campo Santo of oblivion, Death led the way.

Young came they hither. Their sun had barely reached the height of mid-day when darkness overtook them, their thoughts had scarcely blossomed into spring ere Death wrapped its wintry shroud around them. Yet grieve not over your fate ye dead who died so young! For morning is the grace of the day, and life's sweetest roses crown the locks of spring. But evening bears the mark of sorrow upon its darkening brow, and autumn is the time of farewell when the swallows of joy depart.

Ye sleep in the royal sepulchre of a bygone world, in the Pantheon of the human soul, the crumbling city walls of old Rome protect your shelter, and beyond, the Campagna spreads its vast silence around your dreams. Ye sleep in pagan earth, a breath from the Elysian fields rustles through the cypresses which guard your graves, and the imperishable beauty of Hellas and Rome veils the sombre majesty of death.

Death is not the skeleton, who, menacing, wanders from home to home in the twilight of paganism, who in the mediæval night dances his grim Dance of Death round the revels of the festal hall and in the frescoes of the cloister walls, and, scythe in hand, keeps watch by the tombs of the Renaissance. Death is a graceful boy with flower-crowned locks and dream-heavy forehead, beautiful as the Genius of Love. Gently he extinguishes the light of life in the smouldering torch he treads underfoot.

The grave is not the dark abode of corruption, polluted by the decay of the body. The grave is the urn wherein the memory of a human soul is laid.

And the wanderer loves to linger amongst the graves at Porta San Paolo. The stranger amidst the restless throng of the day seeks refuge with ye, silent strangers, who for good and all have stayed behind in old Rome. From far come friendly thoughts to your sweet Campo Santo, where forgetfulness and peace live among cypresses and roses.

The twilight of dreams falls over Rome, and the afterglow of antiquity lights up the solemn ruins. Like the bas-relief of an old sarcophagus, the summer of Italy enshrines the strangers' rest.

CHAPTER XVI

INSTEAD OF A PREFACE

XVI

INSTEAD OF A PREFACE

HE WHO has written this little book is no author: his life belongs to reality and does not leave him any peace for indulging in fiction, and besides, he has for over twenty years limited his best thoughts and efforts to that special authorship which has the apothecaries for its only public. He knows very well that there is "too much Ego in his Cosmos," that there is too much of the writer himself in these pages. He has honestly tried his best to remediate this defect, but he has failed; in vain will the reader from the first chapter to the last try to shake off this vague personality.

Now I want to tell you of a little incident in my professional career which, to a considerable extent, influenced my determination to publish this book. One day I found sitting in my consulting-room a young lady with a huge parcel on her knees. I asked her what I could do for her, and she began by telling me a long tale of woe about herself. She said that nothing interested her, nothing amused her, she was bored to death by everything and everybody. She could get anything she wished to have, she could go anywhere she liked, but she did not wish for anything, she did not want to go anywhere.

Her life was passed in idle luxury, useless to herself and to everybody else, said she. Her parents had dragged her from one physician to another: one had prescribed Egypt, where they had spent the whole winter; another Cannes, where they had bought a big villa; a third India and Japan, which they had visited in their fine yacht. "But you are the only doctor who has done me any good," she said. "I have felt happier during this past week than I have been for years. I owe it to you, and I have come to thank you for it." She began rapidly to unfasten her parcel, and I stared at her in amazement while she produced from it one big doll after another, and quite unceremoniously placed them in a row on my writing-table amongst all my books and papers. There were twelve dolls in all, and you never saw such dolls. Some of them were dressed . in well-fitting tailor-made jackets and skirts; some were evidently off for a yachting trip in blue serge suits and sailor hats; some wore smart silk dresses covered with lace and frills, and hats trimmed with huge ostrich feathers; and some looked as if they had only just returned from the Queen's drawing-room.

I am accustomed to have queer people in my

consulting-room, and I thought I noticed something glistening in her eyes.

"You see, doctor," said she with uncertain voice, "I never thought I could be of any good to anybody. I used to send money to charities at home, but all I did was to write out a cheque, and I cannot say I ever felt the slightest satisfaction in doing so. The other day I happened to come across that article about Toys in an old *Blackwood's Magazine,* and since then I have been working from morning till evening to dress up all these dolls for the poor children you spoke about. I have done it all by myself, and I have felt so strangely happy the whole time."

And I, who had forgotten all about this little escapade from the toil of my everyday life, I looked at the sweet face smiling through the tears, I looked at the long row of dolls who stared approvingly at me from among my medical paraphernalia on the writing-table. And for the first and last time in my life did I feel the ineffable joy of literary triumph, for the first and last time in my life did I feel that mystic power of being able to move others.

Her carriage was waiting for her at the door, but we sent it away, and I put the kind donor and some of her dolls in a cab, and I remember we went to see Petruccio. I could see by her shyness that it was the first time she had entered the home of the poor. She gave each child a magnificent doll, and she blushed with delight when she saw the little sisters' beaming faces and heard the poor mother's "God bless you!" Hardly had a week passed before she brought me another dozen of dolls, and twelve more sick and destitute children forgot all about their misery. At Christmas I got up a big festa in the Jardin-des-Plantes quarter, where most of the poor Italians live, and the Christmas-tree was loaded with dolls of all sizes and descriptions. She went on bringing me more and more dolls, and there came a time when I did not know what to do with them, for I had more dolls than patients. Every chair and table in my rooms was occupied by a doll, and people asked me to show them "the dear children," and when I told them I was a bachelor and had not got any, they would not believe me. To tell you the truth, when spring came I sent the lady to St. Moritz for change of air. I have never seen her since, but should she come across this book she may know that it was she and her dolls who first made me think of publishing it.

There is nothing like success. Some time ago I received a letter from a man I never heard of, who wrote me that he was the mayor of a large town. He said that after having read a little paper called "For those who love music," he had revoked the order which forbade organ-grinders to play in the streets of his town, and had told his children always to give the old man a penny, for "perhaps it is Don Gaetano!" I admit I was very much flattered by this, and no doubt, the kind mayor has also been instrumental in my bringing out this little book.

I have been waiting in vain for a letter from the Germans in Capri; when I hear from them my literary ambition will have reached its zenith, and I shall relapse into silence again.

CPSIA information can be obtained at www.ICGtesting.com
Printed in the USA
BVOW010144201212

308657BV00005B/720/P